There is one religion:

The Religion of KNOW THYSELF.

Knowing the elements of one's identity helps one in becoming a structured self, only then this self can move toward a state of wholeness and selflessness.

This book attempts to answer those seemingly ordinary questions of life, with deep factual/practical answers. How do I get to my core being? Who am I? What do I do with my religion, culture, environment, family, gender, childhood etc., and how should I interact with these aspects of my identity? I feel like I have no use for some of these concepts. Do I need to learn about them, and if so, why? How do I put a meaning to my life? What do I do with my emotional baggage? Others say I have it all, so why do I feel empty, sometimes? Why do I have such an emotional pain and can't cure it? I have so many people around me, so why do I feel lonely sometimes?

In this book there is a case example of an individual who learned about her culture, religion, and family background to ease her self-growth process. An individual who used her immigration experience as a blessing, considering herself privileged to have had experienced living in two seemingly different countries in her lifetime, she moved from East to West in her teen life. She came to learn that this experience had expanded her mind, and thought in ways that would not have been possible if she had not immigrated. She also learned ways to learn and acknowledge the aspects of her life that she had escaped from, and found the experience fulfilling and uplifting. At the end, finding one's self, we can learn to move above and beyond any conditioning and become selfless. This is where we become a master of our own existence by design and are granted full access to our free will. But it takes effort, discipline and determination to get there.

Note to the reader: Throughout this book, the subjects he as well as she are both referred to as she. This is in no way a matter of preference but of simplicity. In addition, the character of this book, Marry, sometime uses direct quotes from sources which can be found through the reference section

Order this book online at www.trafford.com
or email orders@trafford.com

Most Trafford titles are also available at major online book retailers.

Disclaimer
The publisher and the author make an effort to give valid information to the public; however, they make no guarantee with respect to the accuracy or completeness of the contents of the books published. Science is unlimited, and there are many facts yet to be discovered and improved upon, as the world expands. The information that SKBF Publishing presents to the public can only be used as a personal enhancing device for building a healthy lifestyle. The reader is always responsible for using the information the best possible way, according to his or her unique needs, environment, and personality. Books, lectures, websites and other forms of self-help tools are general and valuable tools for a person looking for self-education, but sometimes they are more like statistical information. They will give us a general idea about most people, but we have to remember that each of us is a unique individual, and treatment for our healing process would have to be administered accordingly.

Printed in Victoria, BC, Canada.

ISBN: 978-1-4269-2653-2 (sc)

ISBN: 978-1-4269-2655-6 (hc)

Library of Congress Control Number: 2010900666

Our mission is to efficiently provide the world's finest, most comprehensive book publishing service, enabling every author to experience success. To find out how to publish your book, your way, and have it available worldwide, visit us online at www.trafford.com

Trafford rev. 1/20/2010

Co Published in USA by SKBF Publishing www.SKBFPublishing.com

Edited by: Walter L. Kleine, Kleine Editorial Services

Trafford PUBLISHING® www.trafford.com

North America & international
toll-free: 1 888 232 4444 (USA & Canada)
phone: 250 383 6864 • fax: 812 355 4082

Contents

Dedication

I dedicate this book to all the people who are looking for a deeper sense of their Being. To all those who do not get deceived by their impulses, those who do not get tricked by the insincere, those who do not slip into a shallow world, those who do not take the phony as the authentic, those who do not take the meaningless as the meaningful, those who do not let their temptations rule them, those who are in control of their desires, those who spend their life to discover and to make improvements for themselves and for their surroundings. I dedicate this book to humanity in its true form.

I also dedicate this book to my two sons, who have been a lesson of love.

Author's Note

As a person whose educational background is in biology and psychology, and who has been interested in investigating culture, religion, and diverse scientific areas with the intention of learning about myself, my place in the world, others, and the meaning of life; I have come to realize that the more we learn and implement the laws and rules of life and its design, the more confident we become in our roles as beings. I have also come to realize that free will is not does not mean we have a free pass to life, accessing free will takes work. The more we work for it and learn to walk toward it, the more access we can have. We can get to a point where we are the master of our own existence and not slaves of our conditioning.

By confidence, I don't mean the sort of egoistic confidence, but a more naturalistic one. This is because in this learning process we are constantly expanding our minds with miscellaneous, yet parallel, knowledge of the world and our place in it. We see others and ourselves as partially mysterious, yet amazing, creatures who should be valued, nurtured, and attended to, according to their degree of valuing themselves and their surroundings. It is, after all, a reflective process. We are each unique beings who have weaknesses, strengths, limitations, potentials, and obstacles to overcome; we are all beings who are responsible for our emotional, intellectual, and spiritual progress in life. If we take our powers for granted, the river of our being turns into nothing more than a pond full of toxins. A river is a river with life and beauty, if it flows. If it can't flow, it loses its nature of being a river.

We can learn techniques to face each challenge and weakness, using reason rather than impulse. Tools and techniques are just what they seem: ways for us to figure out how to overcome problems and to mature. These tools are very personal, and should be molded according to our individual needs and levels of maturity. For example, we cannot expect a first grader to solve a problem the same way we expect an educated thirty-year-old person to do it, they have different levels of understanding and intellectual maturity and should be viewed as such.

Mentally and spiritually, we are at different levels of maturity. It is not related to age. It is related to how well we have been able to divest ourselves of the hindrances to maturity, and how well we have been able to learn who we are: our identity. It is also related to how well we have been able to discover our emotional side, our feelings, our behaviors, our thoughts, and our reactions to situations. Change is a must in the process of life, changing that comes from an intention to improve not because of instability. Changing toward expansion, just like the universe itself is expanding, so shall we.

The journey of life will continue until the day that we each take our last breath. After that, we will step into the mysterious. I call it "mysterious," because, as yet, it has not been scientifically discovered. In general, a mystery is an explanation for something which is unbelievable, unfamiliar, or unexplainable according to the knowledge available at the time. Something that was considered mysterious one hundred years ago might be ordinary knowledge today.

This book is dedicated to those who want to work on the process of self-discovery. Every segment of this book has been the result of my exploration, search, education, and personal experiences. I will use a character in this book and will name her Marry. It should be noted that Marry's character is a counselor herself, and that is the reason she is familiar with many of the psychological concepts for self growth. Marry has many similarities to me, and many other men and women, but to make sure perceptions are not made into judgments, no one's feelings are hurt, and there is more benefit than harm to the reader, we will create a character for the sake of this book rather than using actual characters.

In addition, it is important to note that in all of my writings, I use she instead of he/she when referring to individuals. This, however, does not mean that I have gender preferences or prejudice. It is just a matter of consistency and simplicity rather than anything else.

Introduction

One of my clients who had come to experience understanding her deeper self, being more of her authentic being, and walking through self actualization process reported the following:

> As I was sitting in the corner of my couch, listening to soothing music, drops of tears came down, one after the other. It was as if they were chasing each other to see which would get down first. It was as if they were happy to be out because I had been holding them back for far too long. I just let them be; they were outside of my control. For a few minutes I didn't even know why I was crying; I just cried. Then I went for the ultimate sobbing. I felt a deep sense of being lonely; a loneliness that I never knew existed. It seemed like some parts of my life, I just had to walk through by myself. It was my reality, and I had to accept it. Then an inner peace and quietness overcame all my senses. It was as if something, somewhere, was looking at me—in me, but yet out of me. It was beautiful and real—not an illusion. At that moment, everything else seemed like an illusion.
>
> This experience is happening often now, more often than before. Maybe it is because I am more aware of myself, my being, and my surroundings. Before, I just used to exist in this world, but now I feel more as if I am truly alive. I have intense

> feelings, I am more aware of my feelings and experiences, I feel more like I am living rather than just going through life. At this particular incident, I had a combination of feelings of joy, gratitude, pain, and longing. Every time I get an intense experience my means of expression is writing.

There are steps we take to reach self actualization, I have written extensively in my other books about this process and about Maslow's hierarchy of growth. In addition, I have transformed Maslow's hierarchy into seven levels, the last being self transformation. Therefore, creating a new school of thought called Systematic Transformational Psychology (STP) based on literature review, a combination of some of the most prominent schools of thoughts including Jungian or Psychoanalytical, Maslow, and Existential; in addition to an experiment in a form of natural observation.

To go back to the self actualization process, let me use an example to make this process a little more comprehendible. After all, things in nature are more similar than we think and we can learn a lot by observing our surroundings. Let me use water as an example. Water, if not in a river bed with direction and a path toward ocean, does not flow, and after a while might even get rotten and decayed. A source of life and beauty may turn into a useless puddle just because it did not flow and did not find direction.

A river is surface water which has found its way to the land from a higher altitude to a lower one, because of gravity. When rain falls on the land, it either leaks into the ground or becomes a runoff, which flows downhill into rivers and lakes, on its journey towards the sea. Does that sound in any way familiar?

Now let me use the same concept of water and explain it in another form. We can even do a little experiment with it. When you pour water on a flat surface with no shape and direction, the water will vanish after a little while. Now if this same water is turned into an ice, heat energy is being withdrawn, and the molecules are getting into a more stable and fixed configuration with respect to each other. Because of the polar nature of water, it forms hydrogen bonds between molecules. This type of bonding means when water turns into ice, it positions the molecules into very specific configurations, to maintain the lowest energy state it can get to. Therefore, forming ice crystals which seen under the microscope is absolutely beautiful, it has a captivating harmony and stability. This concept can be compared with self actualization. .

Let me elaborate on that. When we are born, we must grow not only intellectually but also emotionally, mentally, and from core (or spiritually if you prefer to call it that). As we grow higher up the ladder of self growth in all these aspect, we move toward self actualization. This is where the water finds a shape. This is when we become solid, strong, focus, determined, and disciplined. We find our place in life and know our priorities, this is where we let go of our extra baggage to save energy, to move up the ladder with lighter weight, we feel more stable with life, we sense more joy of life for simple things, we learn more acceptance, we don't waste as much energy undoing damaging instead we learn to spend our energy to build, we are less needy and have less anxious attachments, we function less from greediness and instant gratifications. Guilt, shame, hate, fear, and resentment do not control our life, and we sense a healthier connection with the bigger picture of life. Love comes from a deeper perspective not just superficial judgments and categorizations. We learn to look deeper into intention and not just behavior; we become more authentic and less phony, we experience more inner control and in charge of our destiny.

In addition, during this process, we become more aware of our different sides, what we are made of, who we are. We learn to use tools that benefit us and dismiss the ones that don't, and we become more aware of our existence. This stage is where we need to learn about the means available to us whether it is our culture, environment, religion, or whatever else that is a part of our experience of life. To learn what they are, if we need them or if we have outgrown them. And if we do need them how do we use them to be beneficial in our self discovery and self learning processes.

But before we know what is useful and what is not, we have to learn about them. The mistakes we make too often is too reject something or accept it just out of imitation, following someone else without truly knowing why, or because of anger, fear, and other negative emotions. Nothing good comes out of these; they may give a sense of temporary relief but it is not the real cure. The real cure is within each one of us, uniquely. We have the capability to discover what works and what does not. Too many times we become just a follower and do not discover what we behold.

After we reach this self actualization level, there comes another level called self transformation. Maslow reports that only 2% of people get to be self actualized, if that is the case, imagine how many can get to be self transformed. To refer back to our example of water, this level of self transformation is like when the water steps out of its solid stage ice, and melts down only to have found a path to flow in. It is still the same water, but going through the solidification process, it has now found a path and is destined to go and join the ocean rather than staying still somewhere and becoming useless. It is even more liberating from the self actualization stage. There is a sense of unity, inner freedom, and being one with the ocean that the self transformed person experiences.

Again, each person has a unique way of finding it but only through becoming self actualized, one is able to find it. Reaching true inner liberation needs self discipline first. Nothing good in life comes easy, so there is work to be done if one wants to experience this. Any other way beside that is the Ego ruling the person making things look like they are real. Such a person may think s/he has transformed only to feel that sense of inner instability because s/he is only looking for a way to feel secure. That is not true liberation.

This book is for anyone who wants to learn about herself or himself in a personal way—a way that includes reason and love, not imitation and fear. This book is about a journey from me to "I," a journey that is a lifelong process and into the beautiful ocean of the unknown. Once we become knowledgeable about who we are, we can stride into this unknown enthusiastically, and without fear, anxiety, and regret. We can allow ourselves to go with the flow, just because it is the way to go; we simply ACCEPT the unknown as another part of our being. This sense of true acceptance comes only with knowledge and awareness of ourselves and our surrounding. Without these two, our acceptance is motivated by fear, or some form of procrastination, apathy, or some other reason that is not related to true acceptance.

How each person is born, raised, and grows in the journey of life is a beautiful, extraordinary, yet comprehendible process. Once we learn the laws and rules of nature and creation, we have learned a great deal about ourselves. We all have to walk through obstacles, barriers, and difficulties in life. The more we are able to free ourselves of blockages and attachments, the easier it will be to go with the stream of existence rather than struggle against it. Once we learn to learn about life and accept its obstacles, we will be able to experience the grieving process in a normal, healthy way when we lose something or someone precious to us: from denial, to anger, to sadness, and finally to acceptance. After all, all elements of life are reflections of each other.

The most important step for us in the process of growth is to become aware of ourselves. We must become aware of the fact that we are given one life to live. What we want to do with it and how we want to live it is, for the most part, up to us.

We have to learn to step out of our comfort zone and walk into challenges of life to expand our state of being. We have to learn to let go of our dark side, limitation, and weaknesses by processing and acknowledging it. What we deny in us will control us.

In addition, we must learn to deal with our psychological defenses that keep us from reaching our full state of being and potential. For example, one of the defenses we use to protect ourselves from the emotional pain of acknowledging that something is hurtful is denial. We go through denial to hide from this pain. Sometimes this denial goes on for so long that it becomes our reality.

I have experienced this denial personally on so many levels, until I learned to deal with it. When I lost my aunt, who I loved, I did not know how to process my emotions. I escaped into a state of denial, and remained there for a long time, not understanding that I had other stages to go through. Denial has always been one of my defense mechanisms. As a young child, I learned to respond with denial by observing that others did the same. But, as I grew older, and with the knowledge I gained through my education and my life experience, I understood the process of grieving as it was. That alone healed many of my wounds. I was like someone who was in a mud hole, but not aware of it. In a way, the mud hole had become my comfort zone. Once I became aware, the process of getting out was a must, and a one-way street with no turning back.

Awareness can be joyful and painful simultaneously. But an aware individual learns skills to deal with the hurt and pain that the life's challenges bring about. This life is truly a journey. In many ways, it has the same rules and laws as going through school. You have to have goals, motivation, discipline, awareness, follow certain rules, and know what you want, in order to be able to graduate successfully and feel fulfilled.

I remember when I was about fourteen years old, thirsty to know who I was, I was reading a book which gave meaning to a poem by Rumi, a thirteenth century poet. What it said was absorbed into my being like water to a sponge. It said, "...know who you are, and only then you will be able to know what your position on this earth is." In my youth, that seemed like a nice phrase, but it wasn't until recently that I truly was able to comprehend what it meant.

Until we truly know ourselves, know each part of our identity, our limitations, our weaknesses, our strengths, our needs and wants, our aspects of personality both genetic and acquired through environment, our emotions, feelings, reactions to situations, thoughts, behaviors, and essence; there is little chance for us to live in harmony with the world because we haven't grasped individual harmony. Until one knows herself, what she does may be for pleasing others, in imitation or out of fear, rather than from love and passion coming from within.

Sometimes it seems like other creatures know their roles better than we humans do. The fact that we are the most advanced conscious beings can help us be the most sophisticated creatures, but in some ways it looks like we, these complex beings who have the power of thought and choice, misuse these powers to our harm rather than our benefit. We look at statistics. We see that crime, wars, racism, discrimination, and many other trends of behavior that are the result of ignorance are rising. We hear about global warming, and that humans may be a significant contributing factor to it. Stories like these can go on forever. It seems our world is becoming worse instead of better. We can't help but ask ourselves, What's going on?

I used the word conscious to describe and differentiate between humans and other beings. Consciousness is a quality of the mind, which is a reflection of qualities such as subjectivity and self-awareness, besides the ability to recognize the connection between oneself and one's environment. Consciousness is the state of being responsive to one's surrounding. Humans have the most advanced consciousness.

So why is it that we, as the most complex creatures on earth, with the most advanced consciousness and with extraordinary powers of thinking and choosing, can't fix the problems facing us? Why is it that our problems seem to be multiplying with the advancement of technology, science, understanding, and the passage of time? Aren't these supposed to be making our life more peaceful and pleasant? Isn't that the point? Could it be that with the advancement of technology and science, some of us may be growing intellectually but most of us are not growing emotionally, mentally, and spiritually? If so, imagine the conflict that this may cause. Having a tool but not knowing how to use it is worse than not having it at all.

We need to ask ourselves: Why is it that sometimes animals seem to know their roles more than we do? For example, when one investigates a colony of ants (or any other creature, for that matter) the organization, cooperation, harmony, and responsibility that each of them brings to the colony are miracles. This is what allows the colony to survive. They do not take more than they need as a colony and they do not attack any other colonies except for survival reasons.

When I use the word miracle, I do not believe that it is something surreal. Miracle is a part of the law of nature, which has not been discovered by the science of this time. Until we are in a time of complete knowledge of all natural laws, the use of a word like miracle cannot be identified as something supernatural. Because complete knowledge is impossible, due to a limitless world, it is not now or ever that someone can claim that he has stepped over a natural law by performing a miracle.

Besides the question mentioned above, there are many more questions that we, as humans, in general, are facing; questions that have always been a part of us, one way or the other. Why am I here? What am I doing? Why do I have a lot, but feel such an emotional pain and emptiness, sometimes? Why are there so many ignorant people around? Why are we hurting each other, sometimes in the name of love, fairness, and justice? Why do we get so easily manipulated by others? Why can't I cure my inner emptiness? Why does my emptiness and longing seem to go away temporarily, and then come back, only in a different form? Among many other questions.

These are questions we all have. I used to ask these questions for so many years, and started to dig deeper and deeper to try to find some explanation for them. Nowadays, occasionally, when I'm relaxing, I sit and listen to music and look at my childhood pictures. My life seems like a puzzle containing some amazing parts as well as some damaged parts, and some missing parts. I cry my heart out over these pictures, not because I am sad or happy, but because of the way I think of my being and the essence that gave me life. This essence is the only source of true hope for me at the lowest and hardest times of my life—the same essence I feel a deep sense of love and connection toward. The same essence I feel such a gratitude for when I think of all the blessing.

This sense of hope, combined with determination and the desire to help others, are the main ingredients that have saved me during the most challenging parts of my life. When I use the word challenge, I should say that I create them for myself. It seems like that's my personality, along with my state of being continuously wanting to go higher on the ladder of life. With that, there are consequences I have to face, but, this sense of true hope I discussed earlier has come to the rescue when it seemed just too tough to handle; times when I thought that I could not take it anymore, and was at the last breath of my power, I, somehow, managed to get back up as if a power pulled me up.

When I was at down points of life, this intense sense of hope came up from my essence. Again, I would be dragged to the end of the road next to the cliff, but some unexplainable force pulled me back before I went over. This essence is a power that I cannot explain, because there is no explanation for it at this point; there is only experience. One has to experience it to be able to have a sense of what it is. The rest will be imitation and illusion, both of which are temporary and counterfeit.

We have to pay attention to the major philosophy that life is like an onion. We peel one layer, and the next one comes along. It does not end. The world is endless as we go along. Our mind gets freer and more expanded as we learn more about ourselves and the world in which we live. Sometimes, depending on what we want in life, we might face challenges and obstacles, but with the skills we have learned along the way we can manage them. We are still human, and will feel all the feelings of sadness, happiness, excitement, and so on and so forth, but there must be a balance with each feeling and between these feelings. These feelings are tools that are available for our use, not the other way around. They are not meant to control us. They are not meant to drag us into states of uncontrollable depression, anxiety, etc. They are there to give us signals for improving our lifestyle, and to live healthier lives for ourselves and for our surrounding. Too many times we live in denial and do not pay attention to our feelings. We completely shut down our emotional growth and live a life of shallow.

As we walk through the pathway of life, there are rules and laws that we have to learn and follow. These rules and laws are according to the time and place where we live. If we become more knowledgeable about the world, its rules and laws, and our role in it, it becomes easier to accept the world, and accept others. Awareness and knowledge lessens judgmental views.

At the same time, however, we must define our personal boundaries, so harmful people will not damage us. The task to know our limits, strengths, weaknesses, needs, and what we are and are not capable of, becomes easier in time. This expansion is what we need in order to step away from the limitations of racism, prejudice, judgmental behavior, and many other destructive patterns of thinking and behaving that destroy humanity in the name of religion, politics, culture, traditions, nations, family values, and so on. It seems like we grab onto anything, making it look positive, to look and feel superior one way or the other. This illusion of superiority can only have devastating effects creating small mindedness, misuse of power, and abuse of our surroundings.

The second philosophy we have to pay attention to is that we have to develop physically, intellectually, emotionally, and spiritually. We see too many people who develop in one but not the other, therefore turning into a human being who is in conflict with herself. Such a person cannot be in harmony with her surroundings.

For example, we see people who are intellectuals, having higher education, but who behave as immature as a child when it comes to emotional and mental aspects of their being. They may compete for a position in an undeveloped way; they may have dysfunctional and unhappy relationships, or have egos that have drowned them deep into their denial of seeing the truth of their wholeness. We may see wealthy people whose wealth has added nothing to their process of wholeness but an inflated sense of self importance. Education and wealth are great tools if we know how to use them to our core's benefit, to advance, to grow, and to make a change in this world for the better; a real change.

Another example is a so-called religious person who has learned all there is to know about spiritual and religious practices, but fails to practice what she preaches because she has failed to grow her other aspects of being like her intellectual side etc. One can preach all she wants, but until she learns to apply what is being preached to herself, she is nowhere near her full state of being. It is simply imitation, habit, and a thirst for some personal gain whether it is money, power, attention, etc. We, humans, can be mysterious creatures and it can get complicated to understand the intention behind a behavior. It takes practice to learn to overlook the behaviors and look at the intention that brought about the behavior.

Another factor to consider is that there are stages in all the areas listed above, which are physical, intellectual, emotional, and spiritual. So, each stage has its own stages. Failure in one stage of maturation will continue and cause deficiencies in the next stage, and in other areas of the person's being. Therefore, we can say that blockages and fixations in one stage are collective. For example, I learned that I had washed away some childhood events from my memories, because I was encouraged not to talk about problems, and "to be thankful, no matter what." This directive was given to me by the people in my environment, who were unaware that when an individual has to deal with alarming conditions as a child, she may, later on, be unable to find the middle ground as easily as someone who did not have as many obstacles early on, if she does not learn ways to bring these experiences out to surface and process them.

Research suggests that babies who do not have the proper care from a caregiver may have a harder time connecting with others when they step into adulthood. However, there is a likelihood that, along the way, the potency of human strength of mind, genetic predispositions, the mysterious and undiscovered (which we will call the spirit), and character can burst into flames and help defeat any shortcomings. This phenomenon has definitely saved me many times over the course of my life; I can feel it.

I learned that I needed to acknowledge my repressed memories, and process them within and with myself. It can also be beneficial to bring in those people who were a significant part of the experience, if they are willing to admit to their role in the process, and their mistakes.

I am not implying that I had an awful childhood. In many aspects, I had a better childhood than many people around me. It wasn't perfect, but then, what is? I think most of us have had negative aspects of our childhood that we need to acknowledge in order to make sure they are not, in any way, blocking us from full growth.

To understand the process of mental maturation throughout development, it's helpful to look at "Stages of Growth for Children and Adults," based on Pamela Levine's work. She saw development as a spiraling cycle, rather than as stages through which we pass, never to visit again. I also recommend that the reader consider Erickson's concepts of development, in which he discusses the stages from infancy to late adulthood (1). This book will refer frequently to Erickson's stages of development.

In this book, I will, among other things, use a character named Marry to explain the different components that allowed her to comprehend and acknowledge the being that she is: one that is going through an infinite process. Marry will be used to explain how she used the different parts of how she identified with her identity, which include environment, culture, role, religion, etc. to recognize them, learn from them, process them and move forward with them.

Identity Awareness

Why do I need to become aware of my identity? What is this identity, and how do I discover it? I think I know myself, but how do I know I am right?

Many different components form what we commonly refer to as our identity. The word identity is defined in the dictionary as individuality, uniqueness, characteristics, self, personality, and character. (2)

Identity is a term that is used to make an individual's understanding of herself comprehensible giving her the ability to acknowledge herself as a distinct unit. Identity may be distinct from the conception of self. The term identity can also mean the individual's capability to reflect herself, and the degree of self-awareness she has. Self-image, which is an individual's outlook or mental model of herself, can also be categorized as relating to personal identity. Identity is who we are, according to our personality, family, culture, religion, environment, surrounding, and our true essence. Many of these are unknown to many of us in their true meaning.

In order to understand one's identity, we need to comprehend what self-actualization is. In psychology, the term self-actualization is defined as the growth of an organism, according to its maximum potential. A person is unlikely to get to this level until her basic needs are met. A person who has reached self-actualization possesses certain characteristics and behaviors. Commonly, these qualities include embracing reality and facts rather than denying truth, even if it means having to stand alone in her beliefs, being spontaneous, showing interest in solving problems (either personal or other's problems), lacking prejudice, and being accepting of oneself and others. A self-actualized person is one who maximizes her potential according to her own needs and values, not according to what others think about her.

To refer this back to this book's character, Marry, she reported the following:

> In my teenage years, and for many years after, I was longing for the moment when I could sense this self-actualization, but I was not able to make progress until recently. During my mental and emotional progression time, I had peak experiences that were so intense that I lost all sense of self and found myself in the flow of the event. I also changed my views dramatically regarding needing to please everyone, idealizing those who were far from being what I had made of them in my mind, caring more about what others thought of my way of life rather than what made me happy, and going back and forth with regard to my goals. All of these came about when I started to trust and truly like myself more, to acknowledge my emotional/physical/mental needs, and to respect my true needs instead of my impulses.

As we walk through the process of self discovery and growth, trying to become more self-actualized, it's worth noting that we have needs throughout this process that we need to attend to. Some people outgrow their basic needs, but some spend a lifetime achieving them and move no further. It is also important to distinguish our needs from our desires. Needs are what we should have to grow physically, mentally, emotionally, and spiritually. Desires are just what we want but are not necessary for our growth process. Sometimes a desire has more cost than benefit and we need to be able to control our impulses to be able to respond productively to our desires. Otherwise they would waste too much of us.

To refer back to needs, according to psychologist Abraham Maslow, people's needs range from lower to higher. Lower level needs must be attended to first, in order for the higher ones to be satisfied. If one of the lower ones can't be satisfied, then the individual has to find healthy ways to replace this need. I explained this concept in detail in my other books, ***Rumi & Self Psychology (Psychology of Tranquility)*** and ***Sara's Therapy: The Way to Purity.*** Maslow states that eventually a person, step by step, needs to reach self-actualization, which by itself is a need of the higher level (4)

To use an example, a woman I knew was talking about her marriage. She identified her marriage as "very happy" and said that her husband really loved her. This woman's need, at that stage of her life, was to have a source of financial and physical security, or perhaps a sense of belonging and of being viewed as a married woman in her community. She did not seem to be aware of her emotional and spiritual needs at the time, and defined them in a very immature fashion.

When asked what made her think that way about her marriage, she replied, "Because he has sex with me three times per week, even if I don't want to. He will force me into doing it because he misses me."

Another one of her examples of a good marriage was that he provided food and clothing for her, and that when he fights with her, he will buy her a gift.

As one can see through this example, this woman's definition of love and a good marriage might be another woman's definition of misery, depending on what each woman's needs and growth level are at the time.

Therefore, we can't define happiness for anyone but ourselves. "Happiness" is in the eye of the beholder, depending on the mental or emotional maturity level and the stage of need fulfillment of the person, which affects the way she perceives events.

If a basic need, like financial security, for example, is being met, the woman may feel satisfied with her life if she has no plans to move further. Now, it is important for a human being to learn to be able to learn skills to be content at each stage of her lifelong self-discovery process, and while walking through the process of self-growth, to be able to function fully at any given time.

Another story I remember, related to this, is a story told to me by my colleague. She said that she was raised in a very rich family back in the Middle East. Her dad was a physician, and they had servants and a chauffer. She reported that her mom was always unhappy with life and complained a lot, mostly because of the conflicts she had with her husband. They couldn't communicate and had no "harmony" emotionally.

The family had an old servant who was a hard-working woman. She worked for them every day from early morning hours to late afternoon. When she went home, her husband would beat her, take the money she earned from her, and used most of it for drugs. This lady did not have any children. My colleague was amazed that despite this servant's seemingly unbearable life, she looked much happier than her mother. One day she asked the servant why she was so happy. The servant replied, "Every night when I go home, get beaten up, and my money is taken from me, I go to the roof. I watch the sunset, drink a cup of tea and relax for half an hour. This gives me hope for tomorrow."

This is what we all need: something to look forward to, something to give us hope, something to give us meaning. The higher we go up the ladder of wisdom and self-growth, and the closer we get to the process of self-actualization, the more the nature of this hope will intensify; but again, it will always be personal. It will become more of a seemingly true and deep hope, rather than a false and superficial one, but we should always find ways to create it no matter what level we are in.

Culture and Identity

Is culture a part of identity? Does it help to know about our culture in the process of self-discovery? And what if we are victims of racism, prejudice, or other negative factors, due to our culture? Why should I know about race, ethnicity, culture, etc., and what does it have to do with my self-discovery? Why do I need to have values?

During the process of self-actualization, self-growth, and reaching our full inner potential, we need to learn about the different elements of our identity in order to be able to become in harmony with them. We can't have peace with something we don't know. As said before, this is a lifelong process. We walk through one stage and there comes the next. We need to pay attention and focus on these elements, as close to their reality as they are. We need to learn to see them with an open eye. We need to not idealize these elements to feed our ego that gives us a sense of illusive superiority. We also need to not define them unrealistically, just to have a sense of belonging. In addition, we need to not escape from these elements in hopes that they will disappear.

Even though our focus is on the future, we need to know our past and our origins. Learning about the past will help with the process of healing and self-growth. By itself, it may not be the cure, but it will make the healing and growing process smoother. Without looking at the root, the healing will become more like an anesthetic (drugs that cause loss of sensation to pain or awareness) rather than a true cure.

We don't want to lose our sensation to pain or awareness. We want to be able to feel our emotional pains, to know why they exist, and to start digging in and healing them. If we can't do that, then what would really be the point?

Look at a tree, It has roots, a trunk, and leaves. It keeps growing upward, but still has roots, and cannot survive without the roots. We need to let go of any anger we may have about our past, and accept these events with knowledge and reason. Only then can we let go of mental and emotional blockages. Only then we will feel lighter and more liberated.

In addition, we need to find a balance between our rational side versus our feeling side. Emotions and feelings are reactions to sensations; sensations that many times can come from illusive and biased sources. There are many out-of-proportion behaviors that are rooted in out-of-balance emotions. Emotions like anger, resentment, etc.

As an example, I remember a conversation with Marry.

> She said that some people seem to have angry feelings about the religion of Islam after the 9/11 tragedy. This anger, which should be directed toward the people who performed this act, and not to the religion they claimed they had, could cause many problems for an individual, because there are more than one billion people who believe in this religion. This sort of anger may cause unfair treatment of a targeted group and, if many repeat it, is likely to cause tension in society, endangering harmony, which will affect everyone.
>
> On the other hand, if this same person increases her awareness through knowledge of Islam, based on scholarly information that is free of bias, she would realize that the true concepts of Islam condemn the 9/11 act and the acts that led to it. If one goes further down the line, one is able to see that the original point of all religions was to encourage people to find values for their life and be able to live in harmony. It is unfortunate, however, that the same tool is being used for something that is the total opposite of its intended creation.
>
> Individuals who have been self-actualized, according to their time and place, have brought all the major religions of

> the world to people in order to help them live in harmony with others, and with themselves. These religious concepts are very personal, according to one's level of understanding of them, but they all have one goal, bringing self-knowledge, harmony, and peace, and bringing to and creating a society which has a set of values and goals.

To go back and explain the concept of cure further, we should acknowledge that sometimes one person's cure might be someone else's poison. This applies to emotional as well as physical cure. For instance, sugar is dangerous for a person suffering from diabetes, but the same sugar is useful for a person who has hypoglycemia. The same for emotional cure, one method might work for one but not the other. We have to learn to set aside imitation and be more original finding our uniqueness in situations.

As mentioned before, the physical body, and the mind and its deepest layers, which are unknown but called the spirit by some, are just reflections of one another. Learning about one will help us in understanding the other.

The first step toward cure is awareness—knowing who we truly are, and what fixations and blockages we have experienced. Until we learn who we really are, finding permanent emotional cures would be difficult.

To refer this to Marry, she reported the following.

> As a part of my cultural identity, which is identified as a person's association (or classification by others) as a member of a cultural group, I consider myself an Iranian who has also been exposed to and has adjusted to the American culture. Therefore, I am Iranian-American.
>
> As an Iranian-American, part of my duty to myself is to learn about these two cultures, and go through the processes of acculturation and filtration. By acculturation, I mean moving forward and adjusting to the new culture, while molding the other culture into it. By filtration, I mean gleaning the best from both counties I have chosen to live in, and getting rid of any dysfunctional beliefs and behaviors.

In order to accomplish this, I excavated into my history and roots to gain knowledge for knowing this part of myself. Knowledge is the source of healthy pride (not the ignorant, arrogant, narcissistic way of thinking in which we get into the illusion of superiority); the sense of pride that gives a person a strong feeling of self-respect and refusal to be humiliated.

On the other hand, an ignorant view of superiority is when a person talks about how proud he is to be from a certain nation, but when asked why he feels that way, he has no real explanation. You get nothing more than immature answers. You can see the illogical thinking this person is holding on to. He is just mimicking or imitating what has been told to him by others, or by the media, without knowing why. It's amazing how easily a weak mind can be manipulated.

We all have a responsibility to ourselves to expand our minds, and to expand our understanding and knowledge. Without this, we can't grow. Even when we hear a seemingly ignorant person talking about deep issues, we know he is not really feeling what he is saying. In other words, he is not practicing what he is preaching. We have too many of those around, these days. It's unfortunate to see that many of them have a large number of followers. What does that tell one? It is simply sad.

Today, in the media, we hear about the axis of evil, barbaric acts, narrow-mindedness, terrorist activities, killings, etc., and somehow all are connected to the names of Iran, Iraq, Arab, Middle Eastern, or Muslim. But, when I started digging into the Iranian culture and the religion of Islam, I saw nothing but beauty in its origin. I am not trying to be one of these people who defends its roots in a psychologically defensive mode. Also, I should say that I am completely separating the present government of Iran from what I am about to say. How governments decide to deal with each other is a separate issue here from historical perspective that I am about to explain.

When I want to defend something, I make sure I know enough about it to feel I am being reasonable. I started by asking myself about the possible reasons for the negative perspective of something that seems to me to have been so positive in its origin. The more I investigated, the clearer it became that the behavior of ignorant people who are members of certain religions and cultures, not their culture or religion, makes something so spectacular look so evil. It is the behavior and the ignorance of some of those members, not the actual concept.

My investigation tells me that all major religions, and all historical cultures, have had the intention of being tools for humans to help them live in harmony with each other and with themselves, and to be able to move toward their full potential building a strong and productive society. Their intention has also been to be helpful in humans having and forming a set of values to live by, to function from a core center. Having values gives people direction and makes life more meaningful. Values are subjective, and vary across people and cultures. There are different types of values, including ethical/moral, political/religious, and social. Values are usually related to the norms of a culture. Now, personal values evolve from situations in the external world, and can change over time, depending on the needs of the time. But what it comes down to is that humans need to have values, and religion and culture were supposed and were created to be tools to help them construct a set of values. Those two like anything else should go through the concept of evolution since time is moving forward and with it everything should go forward as well. We can's implement the exact same rules and laws of last century to this one and expect perfect results. Minds are expanding, needs are changing, level of understanding is becoming more deep; and so should be everything else.

Unfortunately, these potentially constructive concepts, in the wrong hands and not moving forward, can be used as mechanisms of destruction. It's like using the laws of physics for destruction, rather than for discovery and the improvement of life. This does not mean that the science of physics is evil. It just means that unscrupulous people misuse it. It is not until the ordinary person educates himself about these laws that he will be appalled by the ignorance of the truth.

Some people, due to their lack of knowledge, start associating culture and religion with the people's behavior. The more they do this, the more racism and prejudice will seep into their minds, causing the same pattern of thinking that started this whole process to repeat itself. It is like a vicious cycle that will copy itself until knowledge and understanding of the root of the problem breaks the cycle and then comes a cure. Going back to the root and understanding it is a part of the answer.

This pattern of racism and prejudice is not limited to one country. It seems to be a worldwide epidemic.

I remember, during my teenage years in Iran, one of my school's wise principals came into our classroom looking upset and disoriented. Pointing to one of my classmates, she said, "This girl is a Jew. We are obliged to keep her in school, but no one is allowed to sit next to her. If you happen to touch her you will go and wash your hands immediately."

I remember looking at the student. She was sad and crying. The look on her face is engraved on my mind like nothing else. I always liked this student; she was one of the sweetest students in our school. I happened to be a so-called popular student at that stage of my life in that school, but I had this sudden need to get closer to this student.

I was always so resentful of the concept of unfairness, up to the point of my understanding. It would put me into a defensive mode, whether it was imposed upon others or on me. This student and I became best friends, and I ended up losing my "discipline" (citizenship) grade, which went from an A to a D in that semester, because the wise principle did not like this friendship.

The administration tried to force me to stop my friendship with her, until my mom, who was a principal at another school, filed a complaint, which made them stop imposing their unfair rule upon me. I was still watched carefully, but the pleasure I was getting out of this friendship compensated for it. I use this example to tell others about the extent of the racism that is happening all around the world.

Racism can be defined as a belief that inherent biological differences between humans determine achievement or superiority, which results in thinking that one's own race is superior and has the right to rule others. One would expect that prejudicial and racist views are declining, but, unfortunately, that is not the case.

In a lecture during December of 2005 by James Jones, professor of psychology and the director of the University of Delaware's Black American Studies Program, he discussed and focused on the roles of racism and discrimination on the American society. "The stereotype of blacks now is one of criminality," Jones said, referring to findings from recent research. "That's significant and interesting, because the stereotype of blacks in the 1930s was one that portrayed them as happy-go-lucky and genial. Whatever happened to that stereotype in the last 40 or 50 or 60 years has changed the image into one that's far more threatening."

Dr. Jones explained the result of a more recent clinical study using Harvard-based psychological tests, which indicated that, "stereotypes live in the mind, and whites' perceptions of blacks are in their heads. The speed with which black faces are associated with bad and white faces are associated with good is far faster than the speed with which black faces are associated with good and white faces are associated with bad." Jones explained further, "How blacks attain psychological health in the face of persistent racism is through a racial narrative in which one finds personal and collective meaning and value."

Now, since a few years ago, the same type of stereotyping applies to people categorized as Middle Eastern and Muslim. It doesn't mean that we are expanding our minds and our intellect and becoming less racist; it just seems like racism changes face and resurfaces. Why? Because the cure was not root oriented.

These types of attitudes are very damaging to a society in general, as well as to the individual members of that society, including those who hold these racist views. These attitudes not only are the roots of discrimination, but also form the basis for justification of unfairness and destructive practices by the people who hold these beliefs.

When it comes to discrimination and racism toward other groups or individuals, any difference could be used. Evidence, however, indicates that we seem to focus more on aspects of stereotypes that are more similar to our most closely held values. For example, if we value beauty, then we may quickly categorize others as ugly, or if education is of value, then we may categorize others as stupid.

There are a number of ways we try to feel better about ourselves and the group we belong to. We tend to think our group is unique, with better features. But in regards to negative qualities, we tend to underestimate them and consider it widespread. What it comes down to is that those stereotypes develop due to little information. It seems like stereotypes exist despite contradictory experiences, and the reason for that is because stereotypes help us feel better about ourselves. Therefore, in many cases, we refuse to challenge them. We may become defensive and protective of our views, and may never even question them.

There are psychological reasons why people become racist. In general, the weaker the mind is, the more black and white the pattern of thinking it holds. This applies to a wide variety of things, including racism. The less familiar and educated we are about people of different groups, the less tolerant we become of them. The more insecurities and psychological defenses we have within, the more projections we will have. These projections can show themselves as racist views among other things. As I said there are many things people do to make themselves feel better—less insecure—about their lack of knowledge of self and others. For example, some like to believe that their group is unique, and consequently overestimate it due to limited information they feel they hold. This stereotyping is related to the process of categorization that will be explained below.

Through my experiences with many types of people in my practice, my seminars, and my personal interactions, I have witnessed what psychologists have already reported: that we as humans put a lot of energy into practices that help us maintain our view of the world. For this purpose, we seek and pay more attention to information that supports our views, rather than looking at facts to see whether our views are reliable and productive. This can turn into a blockage that preoccupies us and takes away our freedom of choice, making us into rigid thinkers rather than liberated individuals.

Marry said, during one of her conversations, that the concept of racism in the USA is not a new concept. During World War II, there were a number of Japanese-Americans who experienced racism and were interned in concentration camps, where they stayed until the end of the conflict with Japan, which had been triggered by the attack on Pearl Harbor.

Another example of racism was when Italian-Americans were placed in internment camps during WWII, or under surveillance.

Racism against Native Americans and African-Americans is well-established knowledge. Racism is expressed differently in different countries, but it is a world-wide concern. It is, however, more perceptible in USA due to the fact that it is a younger country that was formed by the process of immigration, making it a highly multi-racial country. So, it has always been a reality which manifests itself in different forms and shapes.

What I can say, as a person who has had the privilege of having two countries to live in, is that peoples' perspective of what they do not know is a fiction rather than a fact. For example, As an Iranian-American woman who has lived in both countries, I have come to realize that there are as many inaccurate negative points of view toward Americans in Iran as there are toward Iranians in America.

As a part of my discovery of my social identity, I started digging more into the history of Iran. I learned that humans have inhabited Iran since prehistoric times. Persian (Iranian) history, in its written form, dates back to about 3200 BCE with civilized nations. The first Iranian Empire was cultivated with the arrival of the Aryans (or Indo-Iranians). Iran was established as a nation and an empire by the Medes. This empire was the largest of all during its time.

Persian king Cyrus the Great, who conquered the Medes and unified the two kingdoms, created the Cyrus Cylinder which is considered to be the first declaration of human rights

> (Wikipedia). This Cylinder is believed by some scholars to contain the seed of the concept of human rights, which refers to humans as having universal rights and status regardless of ethnicity, nationality, and sex.
>
> Cyrus was the first king of Iran to be properly called so. His seminal ideas greatly influenced later human civilizations. He advocated "love" rather than "fear," and his concepts have been reported to have influenced the US Constitution.
>
> While walking through the hallway of time and investigating my cultural background, I had to wonder what happened to this nation, which was a large, civilized nation when there was no other, that had a well-developed language which is now 2,500 years old, had possibly the first declaration of human rights through Cyrus the Great, had poets, philosophers, mathematicians, and scientists like Hafez, Mowlana, and Abu Ali Sina, among many others who contributed greatly to humanity, had a high rate of educated youth, but is now identified as a barbaric nation.
>
> As I read through history, it becomes clear to me that behaviors that are the result of irrational patterns of thinking in the name of culture, religion, family, and the like, could be one of the main destructive forces behind a nation's deterioration. Acts of selfishness, having no sense of community, destruction in the name of religion and irrational beliefs, extreme forms of black-and-white thinking, crossing other people's boundaries in the name of family values, and many more products of ignorance, leading to patterns of behavior that give rise to destructive forces, can drive any nation toward annihilation. It is not until awareness gives rise to a change that this process can be reversed.

As reported in the previous section, humans have a natural tendency to do what is called categorization, which means that we often put people and ourselves into groupings. We start labeling people as a Muslim, Turk, Jew, etc. The process of identification in which we associate with certain groups can help us with our self-esteem, if it turns out to be a positive experience. During the comparison process, we compare our group with others, imagining a favorable bias toward the group to which we belong. This is mainly because we are used to our own way; our comfort zone. Therefore, we see it as the better way. This is like the example of our mom's cooking. Because our taste buds are used to it, we think she's the best cook.

The notion of social identity, which is a person's labeling of themselves as a member of a certain group (nation, social class, subculture, ethnicity, gender, etc.), is also a state of identity that should bring a sense of pride to an individual. This sense of satisfaction can further increase the sense of community and belonging to a group. Some people, however, will try to insert more pieces into their identity by behaving in ways that have only a shallow relationship to the larger group.

When it comes to identity, some people seem to suffer from what Erik Erickson calls "identity crisis." Identity crisis is believed to be the most important battle humans encounter as they go through their developmental stages. The identity is both a subjective sense and a visible characteristic of personal autonomy and connection, harmonized with some belief in the autonomy and connection of a shared world view. If what is given to the person when she is born is in harmony with what the environment provides her, the chances of being infected by the disease of identity crisis decreases significantly.

According to Erikson's stages, the inception of the identity crisis is in the teenage years, and only those who do well in resolving the crisis will be ready to face future identity challenges in life. But identity crisis may well be applicable to society at large, because of the world's changing demands to continually redefine ourselves. Erikson suggests that people experience an identity crisis when they lose "a sense of personal sameness and historical continuity." In many parts of the world, identity crises are more common now than before, due to many different factors, among which are the world's technology, global economy, immigration, and dynamics in local and world politics.

> Marry said, when I look at myself in the process of self-discovery, I see my self-concept or self-identity as the sum of mental and abstract insights and determined views that my conscious being clings to for my own existence. This sum has

been gathered throughout the years, and is a nonstop process. My self-consciousness, which is the awareness of me from myself, is not the same as my self-concept. Parts of my self-concept include physical, psychological, and social features, and are affected by my attitudes, habits, beliefs, and ideas. These have been implemented in me throughout the years of maturation, and now it is my duty to go through the process of filtration—to hold onto the beliefs and habits that are beneficial to my being, and get rid of those that are damaging. Then, with determination and knowledge, I can go through the process of individuation and learn to hold onto the components and attributes that are healthy and useful for my concept of self-image and self-esteem. In addition, I have to find a balance between individuation while at the same time feeling a sense of connection to a larger picture. I think they can both be implemented at the same time.

Filtration of irrational thoughts and behaviors are important factors. Just because one's ancestors, for example, believed in something and may or may not have imposed it on to their offspring, does not mean that he has to carry that belief with him today. It might have worked for then but may not work now. It is up to us to make responsible choices as to which ones are still useful. Beliefs and behaviors, like anything else, have to grasped and learned, but we also have to adjust them to the process of development and progression to help us be mentally and spiritually healthy beings. Life is moving forward, and so should beliefs and how we apply them to our everyday lives.

Since my childhood, I have been a product of traditional ways of thinking, some of which did not evolve further because no one challenged them. Some of these traditional ways of thinking are still productive and useful, and have become part of my values and beliefs, without which I can't be who I am, and can't accomplish my goals. They gave me a sense of direction and goal; they helped me be more self-disciplined. But there are others that I was continuously struggling with, until I was able to see that they were not functioning anymore, and I found the strength to move out of my comfort zone and let go of them.

An important element in my goal-setting and achieving success is for me to discipline myself. I feel like a human without the ability to restrain himself, a valueless human, is one that is being pulled all around. This human is wasting a lot of energy without any clear direction in a self-created chaotic life. I, however, strongly believe that values should be based on knowledge, not imitation. Just because X or Y did a certain thing does not make it right for me to repeat it, if I don't dare to ask myself why, and get a reasonable explanation. I'm teaching my children to ask WHY all the time. To demand reasons, and to want to know more. This self-discipline that I'm referring to is something that has been achieved by the knowledge obtained from both my culture and my religion, in addition to extensive reading, learning and practicing in the true sense, and from the training I have been able to achieve throughout my life. I still have a lot to work on, and, as I mentioned before, it is a life-long process. But I have come to realize that my being and my life get much closer to where I want them to be when I have a certain set of values and beliefs that I stand for. I become more focused and as a result the ups and downs of life do not become my whole life but incidents passing by while I still work to get what is best for my soul.

Each individual has certain essential values, which are subjective sets of beliefs that may differ across people and cultures. There are different categories of values; personal and cultural. Valid personal values evolve from experiences we have with the external world, some of which must change over time, and develop. For example, it is my personal experience, working with clients from different cultures, that sometimes older adults impose their personal values on the younger generation. The younger generation rejects them because they don't think these values are relevant any more. The imposing person feels rejected and disrespected, and tries to inflict yet another negative feeling onto the younger one—that is, guilt. For example, let us refer back to Marry's story.

Marry said that in many small cities in my home country, Iran, the concept of divorce is equivalent to an unfeasible act, no matter what your reason for the divorce is. I remember reading a specific example which I found very alarming. The report indicated that emotional divorce in Iran is increasing, and that there are people who actually have businesses selling spells to women who want their husbands cursed or dead. The report mentioned that these people's businesses are increasing, and they are making millions of toomans (Iran's currency). The divorce rate in Iran is much lower than in USA, but that does not mean that there are fewer problem marriages.

The example I used above is not limited to Iran. I was watching a program which showed a woman hiring a hit man to kill her husband, here in the United States. When the hit man (who was really a cop) asked her, "Why not just get a divorce?" she replied in a shocked manner, something to the effect of, "What are you talking about? I'm from a Catholic family. Divorce is condemned. We do not get divorce." This shows the severity of the situation.

We, as humans, should have a set of values with which to persevere, in order to be able to maintain a sense of integrity. One thing I cannot deny is that even though my upbringing might not have been ideal, some parts of it have facilitated the values that I hold dear today. In addition, my upbringing assisted me with the process of self-discipline, which is a continuous route.

To be more specific, in the Middle Eastern culture, in some families, a woman is taught to respect her body and her physical beauty, and not to let others take advantage of it for temporary personal gain and pleasure. We were told that 'you are not a garbage disposal." You have to find the right person, and make love when there is a strong feeling of love and future. Chastity before marriage is encouraged; virginity in its deepest form is mostly a state of personal purity. Virginity in most Middle Eastern cultures is closely interlinked with personal and family honor. By tradition, there is a belief that losing one's virginity before marriage is a matter of shame. This concept, if implemented in its correct form, encourages an individual to value herself and her body, and not to give in to instant gratification that may cause physical and mental injury, low self esteem, unwanted pregnancies, STDs, as well as harm to society.

In Iran, although there is a growing tendency for Iranian youth to date and choose their own partners, rather than having the marriage arranged by their parents, only a small number of these individuals engage in sexual intercourse before their weddings. Many Iranian women still hold onto the value that they should respect themselves and their bodies, and that sexual intimacy with a man comes way down the road of a relationship, after the assurance that there will be a long-term commitment, support, and love.

When it comes to having values, and its psychological benefits, a person can gain a sense of integrity if she holds on to her values regardless of other people's perspective or opinion. As I said before, values have to be based on knowledge, not imitation. Having personal values also helps us gain a sense of freedom or autonomy as beings, which guides us through the decision-making process.

To go back to the conversation with Marry: She said that values are personal matters and may be different for different individuals. The way we define values may also differ significantly from one person to the other. For example, an older male in a family may define as a part of what he sees valuable in a woman as "a wife who takes care of her husband and sacrifices herself for him." When asked about his part in the marriage, he may say that as long as he is a good breadwinner, it's enough. If the woman asks for more than that, she has too high expectations, which is punishable. Nowadays, this pattern of thinking may not be reasonable for an educated woman who is not looking for a breadwinner, but is looking for someone who can be an equal partner in everything, including physical, emotional, and spiritual needs. She might view this older man's definition of sacrifice as self-destruction, weakness, and self-devaluation.

I remember a conversation I had with a client who had come home from a short trip only to find another woman's underwear in her bed. She did not even confront her husband about this! Instead, she went into a state of denial, because she'd been taught that sacrifice in a marriage is valued. But this response apparently was not doing this person any good. She was depressed, anxious, and had low self-esteem.

I had to explain to her what the word sacrifice meant, and that, in its balanced form, it is a compromise we make for a healthy, productive relationship. At the end, it has to feel good. I explained to her that what she did was not sacrifice, but escape and denial, reacting to her fears and inability to trust herself. I explained the consequences of denial, which are anxiety, depression, and low self-esteem. She suffered from many of them. At that point she did not seem to be ready to make any changes. She may never be ready, and it is not my job to make a judgment on that. I use her case as an example of how an irrational pattern of thinking, in any form, but especially in the form of values, can destroy us.

Another example that sticks in my mind concerns a lady client of mine. Her husband used alcohol and would abuse her and her children, physically and emotionally. When asked why she did not take any action to protect herself and her children from such a harmful environment, her response was, "How can I take action? It would look bad in the neighborhood, and among family and friends." She was willing to destroy herself and her children to keep the mask on. When I asked why, she did not have an explanation, a reason, or anything to say that made sense. She was finally able to realize that what she did was as damaging to her and her children as what her husband did. Subsequently, this woman did a lot of work on herself, and was able to get rid of some of the damaging thought patterns. She finally took action. One day after trying many other ways that were not effective, she called the police on her husband.

The police arrested her husband for alcohol use, which is

harshly punishable in parts of Middle East. They made him sign a contract that he wouldn't use alcohol any more, and that if he did, he would be jailed for it. This made him stop. The woman was very happy and proud of herself for taking action and getting positive results.

Now, this does not mean that this remedy will work for every situation and all individuals. The ways we go about solving our problems are very personal matters that require attention, skill, and courage. But we have to make a dysfunctional situation better, one way or another, rather than falling deeper into the denial stage.

To also go back to the subject we were discussing before, I talked a lot of the Iranian part of me, and would like to give a brief explanation of my American side too. I came to this country when I was a late teenager, and am likely to spend most of my life in American society. I consider myself Iranian-American, because I am both. I did a lot of investigation of the American culture, to learn more about the seed that was planted in me, to see how I want to let it grow. I learned that the culture of the United States is a Western culture. This culture has been rising since long before the United States became a country. British culture, as well as other places in Europe like Ireland, Germany, Poland, and Italy, as well as other groups like Native Americans and Africans have been influential on America's beginning. The United States has been known as a melting pot, but in recent times it has been identified as more of a salad bowl, as its different cultures tend to maintain their uniqueness. There are many incorporated but unique subcultures within the United States.

If one pays attention to this simple and comprehensible explanation of United States and its roots, one is more likely to understand that the concept of racism is something that will damage the whole country and its inhabitants. One can't live in a "salad bowl" country and yet have a limited perspective and judgmental views, due to lack of knowledge, toward one's neighbors. This point of view doesn't belong in an environment where cultures intermingle. I would say the only person who does not belong to this county is the one who cannot accept its diversity.

As a person who has experienced both the Eastern and Western life styles, I have come to realize that if my intention is to learn, I can have the best of both worlds and be truly proud to be Iranian-American, accepting both countries. On the other hand, if I don't know my roles in each of the two worlds, this ignorance will be yet another factor contributing to the fragmentation of my sense of identity. I have come to learn that one has to learn the process of acculturation, and walk through each of its stages smoothly, in order to be able to accept, respect, and adjust to a new way of life while holding on to the parts of the original cultural values that have proven useful.

Acculturation is the result of the continuing exchange of cultural identities when two or more cultures and its members come into contact. The culture groups may change a bit, but they remain largely distinct. Recent conceptualization of acculturation involves pointing to the importance of the individual's ability to sustain her culture of origin while adopting characteristics from the new culture for cultural adaptation.

To relate this to my personal experience, the Eastern part of me has helped me a great deal in practicing and developing many of my values and methods of self-discipline, which are the main contributing factors in determining where I want to go with my life.

The Western part of me has helped me with the process of individuation, and challenging some of my irrational patterns of thinking. The influences of the two cultures were useful for me to be able to find a balance. Now, this is a continuous process for me, but I don't believe I would have been able to accomplish so much if I did not have this immigration experience. With all its loneliness, challenges, hardships; something good came out of it because I choose to bring something good.

Environment and Identity

Why do I need to know about my childhood and my environment in the process of Self-discovery? Why is my upbringing so important, and what if I didn't have a great upbringing?

The concept of nature vs. nurture is not a new idea. More and more researchers are finding that both these concepts are equally important in how a person becomes a human.

> As an example, Marry said that I, like many people, did not have a perfect upbringing. Mine was a combination of positive and negative experiences. For many years, however, I was in a state of denial, thinking that everything was okay. If you ask someone about her life and she says it is absolutely perfect, there's a chance that this person is in a state of denial. Denial is a defense mechanism in which a person is faced with a fact that is too painful to accept. She ends up rejecting the fact, persisting in insisting that it is not true, despite the evidence.

Humans use many types of defense mechanisms in the face of danger. One of these is denial. Denial can block us from acknowledging that we too may have a shadow, a dark side, weaknesses. Carl Jung said that what we do not acknowledge will control us rather than us being in control. So, it is not having or not having the shallow that matters, after all, we all do have weaknesses. But what matters is whether we are in control of these dark sides or if they are in control of us. What we are not aware of will repeat itself for a life time to come. For example, if we acknowledge that we have an angry aspect to us, then we can learn ways to be in control of this anger, only expressing it as an assertiveness rather than aggressiveness.

Some people confuse being in denial with positive thinking or being positive or always being happy. With every experience, it is important for us to acknowledge it as it happens, process it, feel it, experience different feelings associated with it, and then learn to accept it. This process leads to self-expansion. If we view some negative or painful experience as positive, then we end up being trapped in the habit of lying to ourselves and hiding from our true feelings, a habit that can be destructive. We have to view every situation as it is, the reality of it. We don't want to see the glass full or empty, we want to see it as it is. The purpose is not self deception but acceptance. True acceptance comes through exploration.

For example, a man may idealize an abusive father because he believes that not thinking about it (or thinking unreasonably positively about it) will make the problem go away. This man does not realize that denying the issue will lead to leaving it unprocessed, which may cause damaging inner fixations in his mental being. On the other hand, if he acknowledges that he had an abusive dad, but then learns to forgive him (which is a separate process) the emotional damage will be much less, or even absent, because the healing process is initiated with acknowledgment and awareness.

> Marry said, the main portion of my upbringing in Iran, my environment, was during and right after the revolution, a.k.a. The Cultural Revolution of 1980-1987. This was a period after the Islamic Revolution of 1979 in Iran, where the Iranian theocracy planned to wash out the school of Western (non-Islamic) control and bring Iran's government closer to Islam. Cultural Revolution is the official name used by the Islamic Republic of Iran.
>
> During this adjustment phase of moving from one form of government (kingdom) to another (theocracy), there were a lot

of jagged and violent actions imposed by some authorities, who were taking advantage of the concept of Islam to satisfy their own inner weaknesses and needs. Many rules were imposed on teenage girls, myself included. For example, I remember being sent home from school with a suspension for wearing white sneakers, because the authorities felt light colors attracted inappropriate attention. I remember girls being verbally abused, belittled, and looked down on by the school principal for having their scarves too short, or for looking too happy. I specifically remember the principal giving a speech about girls who laughed a lot and how they might go to hell and be hanged on the walls of hell.

One can only imagine the amount of confusion these authority figures forced upon children, some of whom ended up rejecting the concepts of Islam altogether. As children, they understood that this abuse seemed to be coming from "Islamic laws." At the time, they did not know that these laws were not Islamic laws, but laws of authorities who manipulated the Islamic laws to impose their own irrational patterns of thinking on others.

The problem of rejecting religion because of seemingly religious people's acts is not limited to Muslims. I have heard it from many of my friends and clients who were Jews or Christians, and from other religious backgrounds.

When an authority tries to use fear to reinforce a behavior, the person may follow the authority's rule, but never learn it. For example, a child might follow his parents' rules out of fear, but never accept them. This fear will eventually result in blockages in the child's emotional growth.

To be more specific, when you teach your elementary school child not to lie by being a good model of truth-telling, by explaining to her why lying is negative, by giving her examples and scenarios about what will happen when she lies, by rewarding her when you catch her being honest, and using reason and positive behavior to plant the seed of honesty in her, you truly have taught her to be honest. She will know the reasons for not lying, and her potential for being devoted to the act is good.

On the other hand, if you teach her not to lie by severely punishing her when she lies, and offer no positive alternative, she might not lie in your presence, but that doesn't mean that she has truly learned not to lie. She is responding to you out of fear. In situations in which she does not feel the fear, she will carry out the act.

This reminds me of a story I heard. A couple set off to the zoo, and upon arriving they lost sight of their child. The mother, in a state of panic, ran to find the child, but the father told her that they should go to the lion exhibit. When mother asked why, father replied, "Because when we came into the zoo the only place we told our child not to get close to was the lions' cage. I'm sure she's tempted to go there."

This is a simple story indicating how we, as humans, are tempted to do what we are forbidden to do. It is similar to the example of Adam's forbidden fruit in the Garden of Eden. Therefore, it is essential for us to learn why something may be wrong or right for us and find ways to explore through our unique responses to them.

In every situation there are laws and rules that we need to follow. Some of these have already been put in place for us, for example societal laws. When we live in a society, we have the obligation to follow its factual rules and laws. Law is defined as a systematic rule to gain justice, and to bring harmony in society. Religious laws are usually defined as the organizing standard of reality and knowledge, as assigned by a higher power. Its intention should be to bring a sense of inner peace to individuals and as a result to their society. These laws are intended to govern all human affairs, and include codes of ethics and morality. Now, just like societal laws may be modified according to the society's needs at the time, so should other laws. So, one may ask why so many people wonder how religious believes leads to so much violence in the world?

Life is a stage for our expansion and development. We are provided with devices to use in order to be equipped on this path of living.

Just as we mature physically, we should also mature mentally and spiritually. When I use the word spiritual, I mean the perceived endless part of man's ultimate nature, the sense that brings about the feeling of connection/relationship to something greater than oneself.

In general, a healthy sense of spirituality can significantly help a person to gain a balanced sense of mental health. This spiritual sense is a very personal experience, which can be achieved through self-discipline, self reflection, knowledge, and concentration. This spiritual feeling may include perceiving life as higher and more complex than what one gets through the senses.

> To refer back to Marry's experience she reported that throughout my life, I was always looking for love from others. I tried to find ways to get the love that I needed because my being craved it. In the process, I was unaware that I was turning into a people-pleaser, intent on finding the love I needed from others. This part of me, the people-pleaser, damaged me extensively, and was not productive for my well-being.
>
> I'm still trying to learn healthy ways to get the love and the connection that I need from those who can truly benefit my sense of self, and to reject those who can damage me, due to their own state of fragmentation. I've also learned that I have to love myself first, in order to know what loving others is. I have learned that love is not the same as attachment, and that in order for me to be at peace with myself, I need to let go of my many attachments.

In order to be able to get my next point across, I need to offer my definitions for four key words. These words are attachment, love, peace, and happiness.

Attachment can be defined as a warm bond that forms between one person and another (either a person or a thing). This bonding ties the two together in space and continues over time. Attachment to something or someone that is positive for us, up to the point of letting go when we should, is healthy. But if we don't find a balance in the way we're attached, it may turn into dependency, and go further into obsession, which is damaging.

Love can be defined as an essential element of a person's experience, which can include a sense of affection, an attraction, self-sacrifice, and a sense of connection to nature, other living things, and ultimately to some superior being. A true sense of love is essential in the process of self-identification.

Peace is achieved when an individual's different components are in harmony, a person is in control of her emotions and feels and accepts them as they come, and the person is aware of her state of being and her moments. This is a very personal experience, which can only be realized through a person's knowledge of self and the components of her identity. This experience cannot be achieved by imitation, because something that works for someone else does not necessarily mean that it will work for me. This is why we witness many people going to mosque, church, and other spiritual gatherings, reading all kinds of books on spirituality, and never changing their negative patterns of behavior; or changing one negative behavior and replacing it with another. They only imitate words that are said to them, and try to mimic the actions. But since they don't know why they're doing it, they can never be satisfied by it, and might even be misguided.

We can learn from other people's experiences, and it is always essential to gather new reliable source of information and to stimulate our mind. But we need to mold this knowledge to our own situations, strengths, weaknesses, and potentials. We need to practice with the knowledge or it is just a series of words.

Peace can also be defined as the absence of hostilities, negative thoughts, and ongoing damaging emotions.

The next term is happiness which is an emotional state defined as a feeling of satisfaction. Happiness can also be defined as peace in its purest form. A true state of happiness is a personal matter. The opposite side of happiness is unhappiness, but they are not separate entities; they are different areas of the same spectrum. They feel, however, quiet different.

In psychology, a definition of happiness focuses on three areas: feeling good, having positive thoughts toward life, and not feeling bad. It is a general sense of satisfaction, following looking back at life and looking forward to what is yet to come. In this view, there is no specific definition of happiness. It seems to be related to both quantity and quality of life, which are very personal determinations. Too many people look for quantity to feel happy and respond quickly to their impulses to have a temporarily sense of satisfaction which they identify has happiness. But looking to find happiness though sense stimulation would usually lead to temporarily satisfactions which may leave the person wanting to gain more to feel the same or even less. Sometime the cost outweighs the benefit but being unaware makes the whole process ongoing and repeating itself. The person may invest a long time gaining something for a relatively short feeling of happiness. Besides that looking for a true sense of happiness through outside world can be overwhelming and confusing since there is so much. Learning to aim higher to what is an ideal situation for our soul but being content of each stage is the key to a sense of true inner joy. But again, it goes back to the fact that until we do not learn who we are, we cannot know what makes us happy. We may imitate what we feel is making others happy but that is usually not the answer for us.

As mentioned before, there are principles in life that one needs to be aware of and follow. For example, as children, we need to have attachments to our surroundings because we can't survive on our own. This sense of attachment should diminish as we grow older and be replaced by more independence. This sense of independence is essential to the formation of a healthy identity. The healthier this process of maturation, the more capable of loving we will be, where there is no more attachment then there is the possibility of experiencing true love. And it will be a love that comes from freedom which leads one to feelings of peace and inner joy not insecurity and neediness.

Let's discuss the stages of mental development in order to address the importance of environment and the ability to become not only physically but also emotionally independent. Psychologist Erickson describes physical, emotional, and psychological stages of development in different stages of life. Life is a process of maturation and growth. Becoming trapped in one stage will damage our growth in other areas.

For example, if an infant's physical and emotional needs are attended to adequately, the infant completes her task, which is gaining in the ability to trust others. Therefore, the seed of trust is planted at this stage of infancy. However, if that infant's trust building process is blocked at this stage because of an inattentive caregiver, she may still go to the next stage of an emotional development, but will carry with her bits and pieces of the unfinished task.

To elaborate with an example for another stage of growth, if a toddler is not allowed to do things in order to learn, she will develop a sense of doubt in her abilities, which may interfere with her skills at achieving independence in a later stage. Likewise, a preschooler who does not feel her activities are adequate may develop a sense of guilt that may block her from growing fully, later in life. One who is made to feel that the activities she initiates are bad may develop a sense of unhealthy guilt.

This is a brief description of Erickson's stages. For the process of self-discovery, it's important to dig into these stages and see which one personally affected us the most. This process involves looking at the root of our problems, which is a necessary tool in curing emotional dilemma, and divesting ourselves of those problematic areas.

> Marry said, I started this route for myself about three years ago, slowly but surely, walking out of the stage of my denial into awareness. This process was one of the hardest parts of my limitless path of self-discovery, but it opened up a new world for me. I looked deeply into my childhood, my surroundings, the people around me, and my circumstances. I looked into many memories I had buried and forgotten. I discovered these memories were a big part of me. They always have been, and always will be. I cannot hide from them; neither can I run away. I had just pushed them to an area of me where I could not think about them. That was my escape. I had tried to escape from some of the not-so-pleasant memories, but along with them, I had forgotten many good ones. I started focusing on those, remembering them, laughing and crying with the recollections, and dealing with them rather than denying them. A part of me was so grateful that I finally paid attention.
>
> I went through the stages of denial, anger, sadness, and acceptance. I was finally able to accept my life as it had happened, looking at what led to what, thus ensuring that I was going to do the best I could to take care of myself, my essence, from now on. I recognized that I have only one body,

one mind, and one soul; I had been given one life to do the best I could to get to my full potential. It was time for me to let go of irrational beliefs, to hold onto the functional and reasonable ones, and to go through the process of purification of my mind, my body, and my environment, to feel the inner peace that I, like everyone else, deserve.

I have read a lot about Erickson's stages and have related it to myself as well. According to Erickson, the stage of late adulthood is the stage where, if we have completed our life's tasks normally, we accept death as the completion of life. Erickson believes that the course of development is determined by the interaction of the body (genetic biological programming), mind (psychological), and cultural (ethos) influences. Conversely, some adults may reach this stage and have a sense of despair because of their bad experiences and their perceived failures. What we should consider here is the fact that "it is all in the eye of the beholder," meaning that how the person experiencing his life sees the situation determines its perceived validity. Is he content and fulfilled with his actions and the path of life he chose, or does he have a sense of regret?

People at this stage may fear death as they struggle to find a purpose to their lives. On the opposite side, one may feel he has all the answers (similar to the adolescence stage), which causes him to end life with a strong stubbornness that only his view has been correct. This rigidity of mind can instill a limitedness that people such as this may never become aware of. A limited mind will become such a person's comfort zone, preventing him from seeing that there is more to experience. Such a person is not willing to step out of his comfort zone, because the first ingredient to stepping out of it is awareness. We can't change what we don't know. Such a person's obstinacy blocks him from getting to experience life fully and with awareness.

Looking at myself, before, when I did not know much, I thought that I knew a lot. Now that I am drawn into this thirst for knowing, the more I get into it, the more I know how little I know. After all, we live in an infinite world, and we are such complex creatures with multiple layers of being. It's like the

> box. Once inside it, we think that's all there is. Once we step out of it, we see how closed our minds were. But the joy of being outside the box is indescribable.

In a world of everything, in a world where opposites give each other meaning, in a world of complexity which offers such deepness, in a world that seems to work according to an orderly law; we all search for ways to gain peace and immortality. It seems like these two are the ultimate goals of every human being. By that, I mean ordinary humans, not someone who is suffering from a mental disorder and wants to die. In this world, we define happiness according to our level of understanding of what it is and who we are. Some of us define happiness in terms of having more things, while others define it in terms of feeding their ego. We spend a lifetime trying to gain it, while we may not even know what it means. Happiness is an emotion that can range from contentment and satisfaction to bliss and joy. It is an internal feeling, and cannot be achieved with external factors. We have to work from our core, our central point, and work our way out. We can't do the opposite. The key is inside out not outside in.

Another point worth mentioning is the law of opposites, because it seems related to the subjects discussed in this book. Marx and Engels stated that everything in life is a blend and union of opposites. For example, electricity is differentiated as having positive and negative charges. Another example would be atoms that are composed of protons and electrons, which are joined, but are opposing forces.

Nature (creation) also comes in opposites, and without this law of opposites, there would be a state of nothingness. We defined day because there is night, black is black because there is white and vice versa. Warm weather feels warm because there is also cold weather.

The same rule applies to humans. We are beings composed of opposite qualities. Masculinity/femininity, selfishness/self-sacrifice, humility/pride, etc. are all examples of the many opposite forces and emotions that are within us as humans. Marx stated that everything "contains two mutually incompatible and exclusive, but nevertheless equally essential and indispensable, parts or aspects." (4) This statement indicates that the unity of these opposite forces gives motivation for movement, development, and change.

It is the same with our personalities, because we are a product and a design of this creation (or nature, however you choose to identify it). Our personalities have a combination of all the opposites; humans are a combination of everything in nature. Our physiology has all the elements; our psych has a shadow as well as an angelic side. We are a combination of so many things. We have to understand this simple and yet neglected fact. We have to acknowledge and learn that we are a combination of everything and only then we can learn what we are made of. Only after this learning we can be in control of what we don't like.

How we want to use our different and opposite elements to reach our maximum potential is up to us. If we keep on denying that we, like every other human, have a shadow, we are letting it be in control. We can't be in control of what we deny. When we lose too much control over our being, we may live a life in a form that is far away from our angelic or pure side and less than an animal. We move toward our shadow side faster and faster and it becomes denser and darker. However, if we take charge and work with them through awareness, we will open our way to getting to our angelic side. When we are in control, the shadow is nothing harmful, if is just a part of us for when we need it and goes away when we don't. It only comes to our rescue when we are truly need it and leaves us alone when we don't.

For example, a person who has an intense fear as a part of her shadow which may be conscious or unconscious may be prevented to take many steps that are necessary for her full growth by this fear. If this person is not aware and is in denial of this shadow part then the fear will come out and dominate this person whenever it wishes to. There are no orders for it to follow. It just surfaces whenever it can. The fear is in charge of this person and may become more and more intense because no one is stopping it. Now, if this person decides to step out of the denial and learns to overcome her fear, she has to train herself to take charge of it. After determination and training, this person will not get manipulated by this part of her shadow anymore. She may further find the ability to take necessary risks in life to move up the ladder of self growth, something that was not possible with the fear being in charge. So in this example, the fear still sexist but it is up to the person whether it would be rational to express it or not. The person is in charge of it. For example, if there is a poisonous snake it probably would be rational to let the fear surface to give us a signal to run from it.

If we look at animals, we see that each species seems to be identified as having a specific personality trait. For example, dogs are loyal, lions are powerful and a symbol of kings, monkeys are sharp, sheep are passive, crows are greedy and steal from others, foxes are sly, pigs are filthy, cats are unappreciative, etc. We, as humans, could possess a combination of all of these traits if inner balance is damaged, because we are the most complete form of living organisms on earth.

Our personality traits come in opposites like optimistic vs. pessimistic, independent vs. dependent, emotional vs. impassive, adventurous vs. cautious, leader vs. follower, aggressive vs. passive. Many of these are temperament traits we are born with. What this means is that we are more vulnerable and more ready to manifest and act on these innate traits. It does not mean, however, that we do not have control over them if we are given a suitable environment which provided us with a balance in discipline and affection. In addition, as adults we can always provide such an environment for ourselves, we have a choice to do that. In addition, there are other characteristics, such as feeling either competent or inferior which appear to be learned from the environment.

> In one of the conversations I had with Marry, she explained that I can see that many of the inborn (what I came into this world with) characteristics I had were not nurtured by my surroundings, causing me to either not be aware of them or manifest them in ways that were not productive for me. For example, I was more of a giver than a taker and more of a leader than follower in many situations.
>
> Some parts of me as a giver were not nurtured properly, due to a lack of appropriate role models who would teach me how to manage my character. I ended up giving too much to the wrong people. Sometimes, I ended up feeling angry and frustrated in the end. Clearly, being a giver was not productive for me, and I had to find ways to balance it and to learn when to do what. I know now that if I cannot learn to be productive for myself, then there is no way I can be productive to others.

> I have also learned that being a giver should make you feel joy not a sense of being taken advantage of.
>
> I am reminded of the story I heard in my childhood, about a bear that befriended a farmer. One day when the farmer was sleeping, a fly was bothering him. The bear, thinking that he was helping the farmer, picked up a stone and dropped it on the farmer's head in order to kill the fly. He didn't know that he hurt the farmer more than the fly ever could have.
>
> It wasn't until recently that I learned that until I truly learn to know myself, I would not be able to know how and why I am helping others. Nowadays, I am learning more and more to give through my heart and soul not my ego. If I function through my ego, I am only satisfying my own desires but labeling it as giving to have a clear conscious. Isn't that what so many people are doing these days? All ego wants is to feel powerful or secure or this or that. Ego is needy in general and does not get fully satisfied ever. A needy ego can never help others for the sake of them. Maybe that's why we have so many charity organizations, churches, mosques, etc that have gone wrong.

As discussed previously, when it comes to a human's psychology and how one is developed psychologically, psychologist Erickson believed humans go through eight major stages of life. He also believed that humans spend a significant portion of their lives preparing for the middle-adulthood stage. Erickson states that if we go through stages of life as we should, later adulthood should be the stage when we look back at our lives with a sense of happiness, peace, satisfaction, and fulfillment. This will give us a sense of meaning—that we have contributed to life—a character trait Erickson calls integrity.

One might read this and wonder why it is that depression and mental illness issues are rising in older adults, as well as in other age groups. Technology is advancing; there is more comfort in the lifestyle. Life seems to be easier, medicine cures many diseases, yet people are under more stree. Does it have to do with lack of a real sense of integrity? Are we so lost in our world and unable to find our way (or who we are) that we end up hurting our surroundings and people associated with us, in addition to ourselves?

Our strength can come from knowing that the world is enormous, and that we are a drop in that ocean of life, but a drop that can affect the ocean. This drop has everything that the ocean has, except it is small in size, so the same quality but smaller. This is again the law of opposites; we are so small in one sense, but yet so extraordinary and beautiful in the other. This truth will help us in valuing ourselves as well as others. When we learn to value ourselves, we can value others and raise up the seed of integrity.

> Marry said, I see myself working hard to get to where I am today. I'm not quite where I want to be, because I accept my path as never-ending. But I feel comfortable and accepting of the direction I am going. I find myself closer to what I want to be when I'm in a difficult situation that needs a lot of concentration. As I was reading the other day, it's like going up a mountain. The higher you climb, the more difficult it gets; there's less oxygen, your muscles start to ache; there's pressure and other dangers along the way. But if you climb with passion, the hardships of the way are embraced and you will go up with pleasure—a type of pleasure that's incomprehensible by non-climbers.
>
> What can damage one is to think that he is a climber because others are doing it, not because he wants it with passion. Such a person will not end up being a successful climber, but rather someone who hurts himself along the way, often critically.
>
> I used to plan my life according to others' points of view, others' needs and wants, and others' perspectives. I didn't know that it was impossible to make others truly happy if I, myself, didn't know how to experience happiness. Sometimes, I was fearful of being judged, because I didn't trust myself. I was encouraged to act in certain ways to be accepted. I was encouraged to be "perfect" (if there is such a thing).
>
> The concept of "perfect," established by the ones around me, was most specifically intended for girls. My family was a well-respected family in, who had many eyes watching them. All of

us children, especially me as the only girl, were encouraged to look and act a certain way. We were considered most fortunate, compared to other family and friends around us, but our life was not as complete as it seemed from the outside. My mom and dad had differences that they were not able to resolve or overcome; they did not seem to be able to fulfill each other's needs. When I was growing up, my mom seemed depressed, and I felt dragged into what I saw as tension. I constantly felt like I was in the middle between my parents. My dad craved my mom's love and attention. Not getting it from her, he tried to compensate for it through unhealthy behaviors like smoking. I don't want to go into the details of my childhood, because I don't want to cross my family members' boundaries or invade their privacy, but I, like many other girls around me, suffered from self-esteem issues and a fragmented sense of identity because my environment was not completely healthy. I am not implying that anyone was intentionally there to damage me, but simply that they did not know any better.

Many parents' way of disciplining, in this small city we lived in, is termed by psychologists as authoritarian. Parents always tried to be in control, especially by having specific rules for girls. Affection and warmth were expressed only rarely. I craved someone who could show me love. I did get some, but I wanted more. I knew my parents loved me, deep down inside, but had mixed feelings about it. My parents, especially my mom, were strict with their rules. I wasn't allowed to get close to anyone, not even my cousins. I remember receiving criticism for minor mistakes, but not being rewarded for the good things I did, which even as a child were many, from my memories.

A mistake for me as a teenager, then, was nothing close to what teenagers are doing these days. A mistake would have been to talk loudly to somebody, to do something that would be considered minor in school, or to talk back to my mother. Most children in the environment I lived in had few options. Parents did not explain rules, or why things were as they were. Girls were raised to be shy and quiet, and not to stand up for themselves. An assertive girl would be looked down on and judged negatively. Children in that environment did not learn to think for themselves, nor understand why parents were expecting certain behaviors. The focus was on children's education, not on their emotions.

What's interesting is that many of the children who were raised under those circumstances idealize their parents, or appear as if they do, whereas children who were raised in a more healthy fashion are more honest about their feelings toward their parents and their circumstances.

The process of idealization is something that many people do. In psychology, idealization refers to someone who identifies a figure in his life to be better than would actually be determined by the facts. For example, I have had many clients who are children of a single parent, and they end up idealizing the absent parent, imagining them as a perfect parent. Usually, if they get a chance to meet that parent, they are able to see that the parent is not nearly what they thought he (or she) would be. I have also had many clients who idealize individuals who have been abusive (emotionally or physically) or neglectful toward them. For example, they seem to feel exaggerated guilt toward mothers they initially described as angels. After digging deeper, it becomes clear that these same mothers were not attentive to them.

Marry said, in one of her conversations, I learned many positive things from my dad, and have many pleasant memories of my childhood with him, but I also have some unpleasant ones that I have been denying for most of my life. It was not until recently that I was able to truly process the unpleasant events and work on the process of forgiving, which meant letting go of denial and any negative feelings coming after that. My father was the one I idealized.

My dad was too involved with the bread-winning role to be around us much. Since my mom was the disciplinary parent, with perfectionist expectations, who was not able to show affection, I tended to idealize my father, to the point that I molded my personality and goals around the intention of pleasing him. I even married someone I did not want because I

> felt my dad wanted him for me. That decision grossly affected the pattern of my life, and still affects it. I was finally able to help myself and get out of that pattern of thinking, but it was quite challenging. We have to be careful and learn from mistakes, because life is too short to make the same mistake twice and that thought by itself is effecting my decision now. Even though I have been divorced for a while, I am still super careful when it comes to considering a new romantic partner. So, when we take the wrong step, the effect can be lifelong.

The term idealization can also be applied to situations of emotional or physical abuse. Individuals who have been neglected or abused as children generally idealize their abuser and believe that the abuse was "for their own good." According to Alice Miller, the world-famous Swiss psychoanalyst, "Every criminal was once a victim, but not every victim necessarily becomes a criminal."

In order for us to overcome our childhood traumas, we need to recognize them, deal with them, and accept them. The process of acceptance includes forgiveness, because once you come to accept what has already been done, and affirm that you, as a child, had no control over it, you will be able to balance your negative feelings toward it, and look at the situation with reason and understanding. Reason will help you understand that, in most cases, the person did not abuse or neglect you intentionally; she did it because she was herself a victim of the same pattern of behavior, and simply did not know any better.

This does not mean, however, that you will let her repeat the behavior, or that you try to find an excuse for her behavior. This simply means that you let go of the anger and resentment or any other negative emotions you are carrying with you. It is worth noting that some people misunderstand the process of forgiveness and confuse it with being dishonest to one self and others. I have had clients tell me that in order to forgive the person who hurt them, they tried being more pleasant despite feeling inner anger toward their abuser. That may have resulted in the abuser behaving in ways that would have made the abused feel angrier than when the process started. This is an example of being dishonest with oneself, not forgiveness. Forgiveness is an inner feeling not a behavior. It is not something one does, it is how one feels.

If one feels empty of the negative feelings attached to the abuser, then one has forgiven the abuser. How one wants to behave in response to this inner feeling is up to one's situation and the abuser's personality. Some may find it healthier not to have any contact with the abuser at all while others may find it better to have a reasonable contact. It is a personal decision and different for different people.

Forgiveness is the mental, emotional and/or spiritual process of coming to the end of feelings of resentment, hatred, and anger against another person who has done some form of harm to a person. As said before, it is an inner feeling, not a particular behavior. It is a mental process which is a personal experience. The negative feelings, if with us for too long, will only damage us. They will not be productive if they end up controlling our actions. In some circumstances, forgiveness may be internally settled without any expectations, and without any response on the part of the wrongdoer (for example, in forgiving a dead person or a person who is in deep denial).

> Marry said, the circumstances and environment in which I was raised have influenced me, and continue to affect my life one way or another. It has been my view that people categorize you by, among other things, your culture. Usually the perception of one's culture and ethnicity is very biased, because people only have a very general view of what they see on the surface. It's very normal, for all of us, not to know the details of every culture, because there are so many and so much to learn. Nevertheless, it's important for us to realize that there is no way to understand a culture until you are a part of it and have carefully and methodically learned about it.
>
> As an Iranian-American, I have come to see that there is a lot of biased information about both cultures from the other. For example, when I was going through the process of divorce, I discovered that people from other cultures, including Americans, expected Iranian men to behave a certain way (like being narcissistic and arrogant, abusive, and controlling). They more or less viewed these characteristics as a normal part of the culture. I heard comments like, "That's so typical for Iranian

men to be like that," or, "Muslim men are encouraged to abuse their wives, right?"

I had different reactions to these comments. Sometimes I felt frustrated. I would explain to them that my culture and religion were born to encourage the complete opposite of their view—that they were basing their comments on an understanding of the culture and religion from an outside view, based on peoples' behaviors, not the actual concepts.

Other times, I just ignored what they would say, because I felt there was no point in explaining. People have these predisposed general analyses of other groups that are different from them, and the unfortunate part of this is that most of us act and react to these perspectives, not knowing how it affects others, the society we live in, and ultimately ourselves. We continuously want to find ways to fill out our gaps and insecurities by thinking that, in some way, we are better than others. If we can't be proud of our accomplishments, or what positive things we have done with our lives, then we will make something up. It's just sad and ignorant.

I talked about some of this but will repeat it because it belongs here, as a teenage girl in Iran, I did not have much power. But since I also did not have much knowledge about myself, I didn't know about my lack of power. Therefore, I was unaware. This manifested itself in damage to my self-esteem. Having low self-esteem was encouraged in girls back in that city. Girls in many areas of Iran were expected to be shy and not stand up for their rights, especially in my family. Looking back, I can see that I was not emotionally nurtured, but it was not done intentionally. Either my parents didn't know better or they had also suffered from this same problem. I knew I was loved, but the ways I was shown love were not the ways my being craved. I always had this sense of emptiness inside.

I didn't know what it was back then, but now I can analyze my past much better. Today, as I have mentioned, I put on slow music, say a little prayer, bring out my childhood pictures, and look at them. I release my pent-up emotions. I cry, I laugh, I feel my feelings and respect them and acknowledge them.

This is very different from the "me" I used to be. I used to wear a big mask over my face, wanting to look perfect, wanting to please others, sometimes burning inside, but pretending to be happy, acting opposite to what my being was longing for, and basically lying to myself, ignoring my true self and harming it. Because of the way I was trained by my environment, those irrational patterns of thinking haunted me and prevented me from reaching my full potential. A full potential that was unique and extraordinary.

Somehow, during my childhood, I learned that it was okay to be emotionally abused or neglected, and that suffering from it and denying it was what a woman should do to keep her family together. I learned that men are superior to women, men's needs come first, and that for a woman to say she has a need is viewed negatively. Most of the women around me seemed to be in this situation, and they seemed to be surviving.

Emotional abuse was and still is difficult to name or even talk about. In my small city in Iran, and in my family there, many women still are not able to understand it, and are not ready to hear it. They wonder if it's a serious problem, because you can't see it, like you see bruises or broken parts of the body. Even if they report it, they will not be taken seriously and will then be labeled as someone who is unappreciative of life.

So, during my upbringing, I longed to please my dad by making him feel happy and proud of me. My life was planned according to what made him happy. And the sad part is that now I can look back and see what a mistake I made. I wasn't making him happy, and I was making myself unhappy. In a way, I can see that I was rewarding his irrational views by following them. Not only did that need to please him hurt me, but, in the long run, it damaged the very thing I was trying to hold on to—my relationship with my father—because once I decided to walk out of pleasing him and into providing what I needed for myself, he could not understand it. I'm specifically talking about when I decided to get a divorce.

Today, I'm going through the process of de-idealization of my father. I'm trying to do it in a way that is the least shocking to him, but it's an extremely hard process of undoing. He just does not want to accept the fact that I am separate from him, and have my own beliefs and ideas about life.

For example, he thinks that I should go back to my former marriage. He said, "I know of many women who had it much worse. They were miserable, but they stayed in the marriage because it is not a good act in our culture to get a divorce." He didn't really have an explanation for his belief. He just thought that divorce was not a good act. My father has also rejected my recent individuation process, which should have happened much earlier in my life. It is interesting because now that he knows I am serious, he is actually supporting me.

Another part of my self-discovery involved looking back at my life during the time I was married. When I married my husband at a very young age, I felt that something was wrong with my relationship, but didn't know how to describe it. It was as if I was far away from him, I was in no way attracted to him, and was always pretending. I didn't even know him well before marrying him. I call it emotionally arranged, since I wasn't physically forced to marry him, but emotionally I did not feel like I had any other choice. I mostly did it to please my father and to escape the pressure the governmental shift and the revolution was creating at the time. If I did one small thing that was different from my dad's view of an "ideal" or "perfect" girl, I would sense a deep feeling of rejection and guilt that were unbearable to me. I leaned on my dad for the affection I was not able to receive from my mom, but found that the cost was too high.

During the self-discovery process, at the last stage of my grieving process, for not having an ideal childhood environment; I have come to realize that there is no such a term, nothing is idea. I went through denial, anger, sadness, and now I am accepting all of it. I have recently learned what it means to forgive. I am in peace with it all.

Marry used the word "perfect." Perfection is a state of being that is not accomplishable, and aiming for it can make us feel hopeless, which leads to a state of anxiety. The word "perfection" is drawn from the Latin word "perfection," which is rooted back to a word which means "to finish," or "to bring to an end." So, this word literally means to finish it.

When it comes to humans, we might ask what it means to be perfect and to be finished. It seems like we can't use this word because when we finish one stage of life, the next one comes. It seems like an infinite route. So, what is this perfection we're looking for? Is it just an illusion?

> Marry said, during my marriage I felt subtly controlled, one way or the other. I did not feel valued. I got mixed messages. I felt blamed for everything that went wrong. I believed that I did everything I could to please my partner and to please others. I never felt love or attraction toward my partner, which is very sad. I made excuses for my partner's behaviors, I felt anxious, and there were many more things that were going on that affected me emotionally and spiritually. My intent in discussing this is not to elaborate on the negative characteristics of a particular individual, but to show my role in the relationship and how it affected me. The damage I received during my marriage is now being repaired, but I have a long way to go. I sensed being trapped in a state of mind that grieved for rising further, but I just could not. My irrational pattern of thinking and my immature sense of self allowed others to take advantage of me (intentionally or unintentionally). I saw myself as a victim, but I don't believe that any more. I think that, most of the time, we volunteer to become victims, due to lack of knowledge of our potential, and of the beauty we have in our design as human beings.

Studies show that those who are identified as victims in situations have certain characteristics in common. They all seem to have an increased perception of personal vulnerability, the view that the world is not significant, important, or understandable, and a negative perception of themselves. (5) Therefore, it follows that if we feel unhappy about the fact that we have been a victim of something, we can change the personal characteristics and views that led us into becoming a victim, thereby enabling ourselves to defend against falling into that same trap again.

We are all born with predisposed weaknesses and strengths. The environment we grow up in can either nurture or deprive us. Imposing one's pattern of irrational thoughts on another, emotional and physical abuse, and neglect of a child can all affect how this unlimited beauty will grow.

> Marry said, my upbringing seemed to be normal at the time of my childhood. Now, looking back, I can find fault with it, which I don't blame anyone for, not any more. If someone asked me about my childhood about four years ago, I would have said it was perfect. I think that was because I was so unaware of my life, and in such deep denial. Also, I think I was idealizing things so I wouldn't be bothered by what wasn't working, so I wouldn't have to work on it. It was a combination of laziness and unawareness.
>
> However, at this time I have come to a point of accepting that my parents did what they could at the time. When I grew into my teenage years, I was different from many of my classmates. I had this sense of compassion that was much deeper than that of anyone I knew. I could sense others' pain and would try the best I could to help them. I remember spending my allowance to buy toys for poor children, without letting anyone know about it. I did it because my being craved to do it, and because I could feel their pain. This sense of compassion was my strength. Everybody always identified me as having the biggest heart, and a magnet of love, but my sense of undeveloped self, and my sense of insecurity, directed this compassion toward inner anger and anxiety, because I did not learn proper boundaries—when and how much to give without being taken advantage of. I constantly had a feeling that I was not getting what I was giving. I craved love from my surroundings, and would put too much effort into getting this love. This was true in almost every relationship I had. I would hide my feelings, with the goal of being liked by everyone.

Now, through these years of learning about myself, I have come to realize that it was not others who created my problems, it was me. I learned that whatever happens to me, positive or negative, is a result of what I do and how I act, and what position I put myself in. Of course, there are always those incidents that are truly out of my control, but most of what happens to me is in my hand. And even for the ones that are not in my control, at least, I can take charge of my own inner feelings related to them. I learned that if I look at my role in a damaging relationship, and evaluate the steps I need to take to stop this damage, the outcome is more productive and functional than wasting my life with blaming the abuser/controller/manipulator/etc or simply a dysfunctional relationship due to lack of inner harmony. An abuser and a controller cannot abuse or control someone who is aware of, and in control of, herself. And it always takes two to create a tense relationship with no harmony.

In some ways, my former way of thinking was irrational, meaning that it did not match reality when compared to what was being perceived or interpreted in my mind and thought processes. Sometimes, my way of evaluating others and myself was illogical. For example, I idealized my father, blamed my mother for everything, and often rated people in a black-and-white manner as good or bad. This attitude created some extreme and distressing emotions in me, including anxiety. I also judged people a lot.

Everybody has a set of subconscious general rules that determine how they act in response to life. This subconscious is what I call the mirror, and mine had a number of irrational patterns of thinking, which I call the dust on the mirror. I started evaluating and analyzing these thought processes, based on facts and what they've done to me as a being, to see which ones I had to get rid of.

It was not until I became more educated about psychology and self-knowledge, that I started to practice what was preached. In addition to my focus on myself that I learned, it was time for me to start cleaning out the dust and the filth on the mirror of my being, and to start the process of clarification, purification, and reflection. I knew this would take time, focus, and energy; but this was what my being had always craved.

When an event triggers a thought, what a person consciously thinks depends on the general rules they subconsciously apply to the event. For example, I held on to the rule that "to be worthy, I must be successful at everything I do, and I must make my dad proud." In light of that, I could not let others know that my marriage was not making me happy, because that meant I was "not being successful at it." It could also mean that I might bring shame to my dad or my family if people thought that I wasn't able to make my marriage work. Therefore, I had become the "ideal girl" according to other people's definitions, even if it was making me miserable.

I could not blame another for what seemed to be my volunteering to become the victim of a pattern of irrational thinking that was not going to stop, because nobody dared to stop it. I, like many others, was not aware that my "comfort zone" was actually damaging me extensively.

I needed to get out of that comfort zone fast, my marriage, as my being was in danger, I was getting more and more anxious and closer and closer to my false self. But was I ready to face the consequences, which included being rejected by my dad, and possibly other male figures in my family? They would feel threatened because my leaving that zone would mean changes to their zone. How would they react to that? I knew I would have to walk this path alone, and many obstacles would be in my way. There was a strong possibility, based on what I knew of the male figures in my family, their environment, and their views of women's roles, that they would react negatively. What if they still wanted to impose their views on me, what if they rejected me, what if they attacked me and crossed my boundary? Was I ready to defend myself?

Also, based on my husband's behavior patterns, I knew he was not going to take it very well. I was aware that he seemed to have this attachment to an object (me) in his mind, which made him feel comfortable. Losing that might trigger a wide range of reactions in him. This, with many other reasons that

I will not go into out of respect for his boundaries, could have led him into a range of unpredictable responses, including what he might have categorized as self-defense, because he believed he was a victim. A person like that would explain his behaviors one way or another, and would do whatever harm he could to get the "object" back, by force, fear, and frustration, but not by love. Such a person due to an underdeveloped sense of self, would act out of fear, anger, and resentment not love, and being unaware, would blame anyone but himself for problems created.

We had one of those marriages in which one saw it as terrible and the other as heaven. That shows you how much harmony we had. One's heaven was the other's not so heavenly experience. I was unhappy, but if you asked my husband, he would say we had a perfect marriage, and that "everyone envies us and our marriage." This is the state of unawareness he was in—to both his needs and mine. But, I knew that I was just tired of pretending. And again, was I really ready to deal with all of that?

When I thought about my marriage, my feelings toward it, what I had given, what I had gained, and where it was going, I just knew that I needed a lot of determination, reason, and hope to end it, but it was something I was sure was right.

There was nothing in my life I was more sure of than this: I had to get out of this marriage. I had tried every way I knew of as a person, as an educated person, and as a wife, to work on this marriage. I had used problem-solving skills, conflict resolution, communication, and so on, but the two of us were at such different levels of understanding that the more I tried, the worse it seemed to get.

So, when the marriage was finally over, I felt a deep sense of relief, even though the process of divorce itself was a burden. But, as I said, it was also important for me to determine whether I was ready to walk down this very challenging path. Was the cost going to out weight the benefit? And for me it did. I knew that in a relationship like mine, when the woman forms a sort of anxious bonding with the significant other, the

> controller intensifies the use of his controlling and emotional abuse when he feels threatened by the loss of the woman. In such a relationship, when the woman decides to end the relationship, the controlling person will sense a feeling of loss, as there is less of her available. As a result, he intensifies his abusive/controlling schemes. But since knowledge is power, since I knew this, I started to get prepare.

In many cases, during the separation and the divorce process, since the other person feels a loss of control, he may impose a lot of financial and emotional abuse on the person who is relieving herself from this controlling pattern of behavior. The abuser will try to trigger the abused, and force contact by conflict. The best way to handle this is to find ways to avoid being intimidated. The behavior is then likely to stop. The sources of intimidation could be anything from making false accusations, trying to make the person look like something she is not, putting financial burdens on the person, scaring the person, threatening her, and even using the children as a way of frustrating the person.

My point here is that once an individual makes a decision, they have to be aware of the consequences and what is waiting for them. Only then can they use their reason to see whether that is really what they want, and whether it is something they can handle.

Decision-making is the cognitive process that leads to the choice of an action among alternatives. During a decision-making process, we have to come up with a final choice upon which we base our action. The first step is knowing that we need to do something, but we don't know what to do. Decision-making is a tool which, if based on reasoning, can bring productive results. This is a psychological construct that needs a commitment to action. We need to learn to be a structured, rational decision-maker in order to be able to plan healthy lifestyles and become balanced individuals. We need knowledge of the matter about which we are making decisions.

> Marry said, the decision-making process about my divorce required much evaluation. This process was a life-changing experience—one that pushed me toward a one-way street;

> there was no going back. Because I knew and felt this was a necessary step for me, I could not simply stand still and do nothing. Beforehand, I had my set of "rules for living," many of which were irrational. I did whatever I could to escape my true feeling, from going to school, to being an overly involved mother, to doing a large number of charity work; at the root of each was me escaping from myself. I wanted to keep so busy and occupied that I would not have time to look at my inner pain and start working on them. The more this escape seemed positive and attracted positive attention, the more I was able to escape. For example, I was admired a lot for my numerous charity work. I did more and more of it to get that sense of praise and security from others. This was my response to the inner emptiness I was feeling.

How we evaluate specific events that happen to us depends on this underlying subconscious, or automatic, thinking. According to Albert Ellis, there are a few core beliefs that need to change, because they cause unhelpful emotions and behaviors in a person. Some of Marry's irrational beliefs included patterns of thoughts like, "I need love and approval from those important to me and all other, and I must avoid disapproval from any source."

> Marry added, now I've learned that there are various groups of people with different personalities, beliefs, behaviors, way of thinking, etc. If one wants only to please others, it means that one is escaping from herself, and is drawn into the process of lying to herself. For example, I sacrificed my needs, my beliefs, and, in a way, my being, to get my dad's approval, and to show others that "I have it all," though my inner self was not feeling comfortable with the image I was portraying to others.
>
> My inner self was experiencing a deep sense of dissatisfaction, which was being denied any sort of feelings related to it. This obviously was not productive for me. Because now I know that those around me are also drawn into a set of irrational patterns of thinking and identity crises, and many of them don't even know what they want, let alone know what is good for them

as individuals. Everything has to evolve, develop, change, and make progress as time moves forward. We can't try to live with the exact same set of ideas that our ancestors lived by. We have to add to them and make them mold into today's worlds.

Another pattern of thinking that I had to divest myself from was, "In order to be a worthwhile person, I must achieve and be successful at whatever I do, and make no mistakes." Now, I am starting to learn that I, like everyone else, make mistakes, and it is very likely that I will make mistakes in the future. But, since I came from an unyielding family, who unknowingly gave me mixed messages, mistakes were categorized as acts that you should feel guilty about, and that girls, specifically, had to obey and follow a set of rules to avoid the possibility of making a mistake, at any cost. That meant that many women believed taking risks, individuation, and independence were discouraged. Now, I see mistakes as they are, not as some form of irreversible guilt-inducing matter, but as something I need to learn from and not repeat. And that is not because I think God will send me to hell, but because I will create my own hell if I keep repeating the same mistakes.

I have tried to learn to act out of love for my being and my surroundings, as well as out of knowledge. I think that my way is knowing and loving. I also believe that in order to be a person in harmony with one's nature, one must have values and self-discipline. I try to hold values that are based on understanding and reason, not mimicking others' irrational ways of believing. By self-discipline, I mean the ability to control myself and my emotions. It can be defined as using reason to establish a best route of action that may sometimes be in opposition to one's desires. Self-discipline is motivating!

There are many other patterns that lead us to an unhealthy sense of self and a damaged mentality. We have to learn them to see which ones are controlling our ways of thinking. These ways of thought are not equivalent to what reality holds. For this reason, when these fixed sets of rules, irrational thinking patterns, and beliefs are challenged by reality (what is actual, not desired or perceived), the individual who has these beliefs is faced with a changing process. She may become disturbed emotionally and behaviorally when faced with this challenge. If one chooses the passageway of self-discovery, one has to start the process of purification by emptying the mind of all these patterns of irrational thinking, which are harmful. Our rational thinking is called rational when it is helpful to us over the long term of our life. Irrational thinking, on the other hand, hinders us in the long run.

In the process of life, we should constantly be aware of what we're feeling, thinking, and doing. We should test these behaviors to see which ones are productive and which ones are destructive. This is a non-stop process. We should consciously ask ourselves the following questions: Does my belief assist me or hold me back over the long run? If my belief holds me back, what rational belief would be more likely to help me reach my goals and feel more satisfied in life? Is my belief coherent with known facts and reality? Moreover, is my belief logical?

> Marry said, I can see now that the pattern of people's cultural behavior, not the culture itself, led my Iranian roots into a zone of deterioration, despite the well-built foundation of that nation and its rich cultural history, filled with self-actualized humans who contributed greatly to the world. The fact that Persia was the first human civilization, ahead of Egypt by 500 years, the fact that it was the first empire in the world, the Persian Empire from the Indus river down to the Danube River in Europe and up to the Nile River in Africa; the fact that during the time of Cyrus all the governments of the known world were ruled under one color (for the first and last time in history), the fact that insurance by government was started during the reign of Cyrus the great of Persia; weight, money, and measurements were standardized in Persia, Sanskrit (mother of modern language) was born in Iran before it went to India. Many scientists, poets, astrologists, mathematicians, etc., offered so much to this world. These are something that makes me proud, but then on the other hand an overwhelming sadness overcomes me. How come a nation with such a history seems to have moved backward? There seems to be a pattern of destructive behaviors that appear to be the results of an aging

philosophy of life, ideas that have not advanced along with time and technology, causing people to be stuck in a disproportionate state of confusion between the new millennium and the old way of thinking. This gap allowed extremists free rein to pick and choose what they wanted to believe, depending on their desires and personal experiences.

For example, religion in Iran, which is mainly Islam, has extreme forms. One such group mimics the words of religious leaders and teachers obsessively, without knowing what they truly mean, and without practicing what they preach. They are easily manipulated by whatever is being repeated to them. Another group completely rejects the beliefs and ideologies of religion with such a hate and resentment that they blame it for all the evils in life, without looking at the roots and the rational causes.

Many do not understand the principles that religion is trying to communicate to them. They only see it as a repeating of a series of rituals. Not knowing what values and meanings these rituals represent will make practicing religion an addictive, and many times damaging, behavior, rather than a tool for development.

The issue here is the ability to discern between rational and irrational thinking. Rational thinking is coherent with known facts. Irrational thinking is incoherent with (or not founded on) known facts.

If I see that my belief is incoherent with reality, then what rational belief would be more coherent with reality? Am I carrying a belief that was injected into me? Have I simply become a parrot, mimicking what was told to me without knowing why? Or, should I choose my beliefs based on knowledge and investigation?

This discerning was a challenge for me, and I'm still struggling with it. As I have said before and is a good example to be used here again, it took me a long time to get out of my unhappy marriage. I stayed in this marriage because I had a set of beliefs, which I practiced without knowing what good, if any, they were doing for me. Due to lack of complete trust in myself, I did not have the courage to take action and solve my problem. I was in a state of deep denial, trying to keep on a good mask. I wore this mask for so long that I forgot who the real me was. When I became more aware of the situation, and the damage it had caused me, I tried different methods for solving the problem. When I saw that there was no solution, I decided to begin the process of divorce.

This divorce was a big challenge and a difficult one to overcome. The religious beliefs that were imposed upon me discouraged me from taking the step toward divorce. They generalized the concept to everyone, and weren't able to make exceptions. No one ever told me that a truly religious person is the one who learns who he or she is, and learns how to get out of inner ups and downs (or hell, in religious concepts) and find ways to have a relative inner peace (or heaven, in religious concepts). Only I can find an inner peace for myself.

We are all so unique. We can learn, but cannot imitate others. What works for others may not work for us, and vice versa. Until we learn who we are, we don't know what works for us.

The question that I often asked myself, and still ask, is: if my belief is illogical, what rational belief would make more sense, logically? What changes can I afford to implement to make myself a more comfortable, peaceable person—a person in harmony with her true self, who does not have to wear a mask? A person whose words, behaviors, and thoughts are in accordance with each other. A truly honest person.

Logical means thinking that makes sense. For example, if you said you would very much like to succeed at something, does it logically follow that therefore you must succeed? No. The necessity for success does not follow logically from the notion that success would be beneficial. Or, does it make sense to think, "Because something is bad, I can't stand it"? Again, the answer is no.

Where I grew up, some people view distressful family issues, family member's differences, fear, and vulnerability as signs of weakness, which causes people to hide these issues so they will avoid being judged, which causes anxiety. The result of trying to hide these issues, and not let them surface for fear of being judged, only worsens the symptoms.

Some women are taught from childhood to "smile and tolerate it," or to "burn and suffer, but endure," especially in a marriage. Emotional abuse of women by their partners is evident but under-reported, because of the lack of knowledge of what it is. The magnitude of the damage that emotional abuse can cause is underestimated, affecting a woman's sense of worth, belonging, and independence. In many instances, this untouched subject weakens a woman's capability of providing emotional support and a nurturing environment for her children, and to give to society and to her surroundings.

As a person who was born in Iran and considers herself Iranian-American, and as a woman, during my self-discovery process, I looked at the history of Iran. Historical acceptance of a woman's position in Iran indicates that there seems to be a pattern of decline in some of the roles of women in that society. Even though the role of women in Iran is much stronger than that in other Arab/Muslim countries, but I think we should compare things with their old ones rather than with others. This way we can measure progress.

The role of an Iranian woman has varied from the chief of society to simple chattel at home. Women's history goes back to the Avestan Period (ca. 1800 BCE) of Iranian history. In Avestan, women were held in high regard. Zoroastrians believed in complete equality between men and women, and periodically women ruled over men. During these times, women were warriors and fought alongside their men. The male-dominated Greek culture was both awestruck and shocked by this.

This amazing social equality, at such an early time in history, is reported by many classical writers, as well as evidenced by many archaeological verifications, an example of which is the remains of women warriors from that period, dressed in full armor. Even more amazing is the fact that these women seem to have kept their femininity while being warriors, as the great contemporary German scholar Barirov reports it. (7)

During the Achaemenid dynasty, which was the first Persian Empire, from 559 BCE to 338 BCE, women played an important role in everyday life. Women who achieved a high status had a significant effect on the state's affairs. They were actively involved in management and trade. The Persepolis tablets, which were discovered in the 1930s, revealed that women were employed, and the wages they received were based on their skills and their level of responsibility, rather than their gender. New mothers and pregnant women received higher provisions than everyone else. (7) Many people, even some Iranians, are not aware of these historical facts.

Historically, family violence was uncommon in the Iranian community. It was unacceptable. The community would not tolerate the abuse of children, spouses, disabled, or the elderly. In recent times, many Iranians have experienced the damaging effects of the coercion of holy customs and spiritual ways by those who abuse their power, the loss of family influence, and the absence of healthy parental and elder teachings.

As a group, we seem to have started implementing non-functional, non-Iranian attitudes, beliefs, and values that were mimicked from those of other cultures, without the appropriate knowledge of their validity. Iran, as a nation, seems to have become disheartened, and seem to have internalized a disheartened sensation, which has led to self-neglect. The result of all of this has been destructive. When extreme forms of oppression of a whole group exist, the damage is unbearable. It can affect their sense of self-esteem, cause shame, isolation, depression, hopelessness, and severe anxiety.

Today, women in some families are, for some reason, viewed as having less value than men, and/or as property. Arranged marriages still exist in some parts of Iran, where a woman has minimal say about her future. This is seen in other cultures as well. Marriage vows, until as late as the twentieth century, declared that women must love, honor, and obey their husbands, while losing their name in the contract.

These concepts are not limited to Iran. In European society and in North America not only did the woman lose her name in the marriage, but also the ability to trace her matrilineal descent. In medical research, the male body has universally been the norm. Many more examples like these can be discovered, if one digs through the history of different cultures.

The fact that women and men have different roles is not disturbing, since it is clear to today's relationship experts that women and men are very different, and this difference is a positive factor, if used to build up a healthy ecosystem in which all people are living in harmony, contributing to it, and sharing responsibilities according to their own unique strengths and weaknesses. This difference, if studied and implemented properly and without imposition, can be healthy and productive to all parties involved. It will not be a power struggle anymore where everyone has a need to prove him or herself. It would be a cooperating system.

What is agitating is that some men use the power that was intended for protecting their women to take advantage of them and gain personal satisfaction. This is one of the contributing factors in women's sense of suppression instead of progression. This sense of suppression leads to feelings of frustration and alienation, and that by itself will harm the family cycle. These patterns are observed in many third-world countries. The effects could be life-long, and the healing process requires much focus, patience, and determination and mainly knowledge and acknowledging that this is a problem that needs to be dealt with.

All together, an Iranian women's movement, which involves Iranian women's experience of modernism related to art, science, literature, poetry, and political structures, has been evolving again since the nineteenth century. Iranian women account for a remarkable percentage of intellectual circles in Iran, and consequently play an important role in forming Iranian identity in modern times. Throughout the last few decades, Iranian women have started to increase their position and influence significantly in science, art, literary, and an Iranian cinema.

Ministry of Iran reported in a 1999 study that about 6

percent of full professors, 8 percent of associate professors, and 14 percent of assistant professors were women in the 1998-99 academic year. However, women accounted for 56 percent of all students in the natural sciences, including one in five Ph.D. students.(7) The list of Iranian women novelists, scientists, engineers, authors, poets, artists, athletes, politicians, activists, etc. is growing exponentially. It seems that a sense of empowerment is returning to women in the same sense that existed hundreds of years ago, and somehow became lost, but there is still much work to be done.

Empowerment is a sense of increased personal strength that can be spiritual, political, social, or economic. The empowered person develops a sense of confidence in her own capability. She feels a sense of control over the decisions that impact her life. (8) A person who feels she is being controlled by someone else, and who does not have a sense a power over her life, is likely to suffer from emotional blockages that can damage her productivity.

Emotional Abuse and Identity

What is an emotional abuse? How do I know if I experienced it? What do I do if I have suffered from emotional abuse? How do I know if I am emotionally abusing someone? What does that have to do with my Self Discovery process?

> On the subject of emotional abuse, Marry said, during my time in the counseling field, I have seen women from all over the world, especially from third-world countries, who have suffered some form of abuse. The idea of emotional abuse is in its infancy in third-world countries, but is more well-known in western countries. It seems like a pattern of thinking exists that if you don't see something, it doesn't exist. For example, you don't see emotional abuse, therefore it is not there. In physical abuse, one sees the bruises, so it is easier for it to be recognized and categorized as abuse.

Several definitions account for the reality of emotional abuse, which include psychological abuse, psychological aggression, and indirect abuse, among others. Verbal abuse is also a characteristic of emotional abuse, and its intent may be to communicate a sense of worthlessness. Any relationship that is composed of tactics to control or overpower another person must be considered a maladaptive relationship.

Any relationship that imposes emotional abuse as a means to create power and control over the other person is considered destructive. Emotional abuse ranges from verbal attacks to harassment, belittling, excessive possessiveness, and deprivation of physical and economic resources. Emotional abuse can affect a person's sense of self and integrity, since the abuser uses the partner's vulnerability to impose his beliefs on her (or hers on him) to the point where s/he is not entitled to her or his own opinions or ideas.

There are also covert behaviors that an abuser can use to work on the outside of the consciousness of the abused person. These could be behaviors that range from withholding affection, denial, projection (blaming the woman for the abuser's problems), and devaluing the abused. The insistent pattern of abusive prattle is mixed with kindness to generate conflicting feelings in the abused. This makes the abused person feel like s/he is on a roller coaster, causing her confusion and instability. The person who got into the relationship looking for security ends up feeling more insecure than when she walked in. She may end up transferring her negative feelings of powerlessness toward her children to regain that lost sense of power. The family is then caught in a vicious cycle of damaging revenge.

> Marry said, in some parts of the world, especially in rural areas, many women are identified as vulnerable to abuse because they are not allowed to individuate. Many of them do not know who they are, or what comprises their identity. Women report that being "born female" seems to sometimes be the cause of their having to put false faces over their true selves and their capabilities. These women have the impression that when one grows more than others do, mentally, others may want to step over her because they see her as a threat to their comfort zone.
>
> There are yet other reports of being encouraged to stay in an abusive marriage and in a state of helplessness because "there is nothing better out there and it is better to be in an abusive/controlling relationship than be alone." Some of them report that family members will reject them if they decide to go with divorce, or if they stand up for themselves to make the marriage better.

I remember an example. A group of men were talking about their wives and identifying these wives as good or bad. One of these men said that one of the wives was an awful wife. When asked why, he said, "Because a group of us were sitting and smoking opium when she walked in. You should have seen her reaction! She was outraged and started cursing at her husband."

In my mind, this woman was courageous, and I admired her a lot, but in his mind she was being too aggressive, and therefore was a "bad" wife.

In third world countries, many families where an older woman is abused, she does not even think about reporting it until it becomes unbearable. This is mainly due to her financial dependency on her husband. I remember a number of people who knew their husbands were cheating on them, but, being in this state of helplessness, they went into the defensive mode of denial. They behaved as if nothing was happening. Some took it to the extreme of trying to defend their husbands' behavior. This denial stage was like a survival tool for them. They believed that if they acted on their knowledge of their husbands' infidelities, nothing better would come for them. They were trapped by their sense of insecurity.

My experience of living in this country tells me that in most recent years in the USAt, the sense of male dominance is regressing, due to woman getting higher status and awareness. This adjustment phase is a phase to which both men and women must put focus and attention to be able to pass through it successfully. Women also have to understand that they cannot go through this phase without the men's support, and they have to find ways to gain their cooperation within the process. Again, in any stage, if we get into the trap of power struggle, we lose a lot of potential cooperating partners. We have to learn ways to compromise and cooperate without being controlled or needing to control. That is when we are able to built healthy relationships.

In some areas of the world, there seems to be a sense of guilt induction from the society toward a woman who wants to discover herself and grow. This can even be injected into her through the males in her family of origin, because they do not want to lose their power in society. They see these women as threats. If one of these women tries to leave an abusive relationship, the abuser's reaction may range from arrogant disbelief (I was so nice to you! How dare you?) to confusion (What's happening? I'm losing control of the situation), to bargaining and pleading (I will make all the changes you want), threatening (I will destroy your reputation by accusations; I will make your life miserable), to seeking revenge (I will focus on this to make sure you will have a terrible life without me).

Despite the increased public awareness and social and legal responses in the United States and some other countries about the problem of men's abusive behavior against women, this issue remains nearly unaddressed in the Middle East. No specific law has been implemented to define spousal emotional abuse; neither are civil actions, such as restraining orders, available for women who are battered by their partner. In some overtly religious families, women are taught to "take it because they will be rewarded in afterlife." This teaching is implemented and imposed by men who have power religiously, who want to hold on to their status of dominance in society without acknowledging women's emotional needs and spiritual growth.

There are, however, many exceptions to this pattern of behavior. For example, some religious groups, such as the Sufi, are aware of the situation and are influenced by the true Islamic tradition, which disapproves of aggression and emphasizes harmony, discipline, and self-restraint in interpersonal relationships. In these groups, "family" is viewed as an ecological unit in which each member is expected to take certain roles and responsibilities according to his or her own identity, values, beliefs, and environment to make a healthy system of cooperation and support (physical, emotional, spiritual, and financial) and a place to nurture healthy children.

The impact of emotional abuse on identity formation and self-discovery should be taken into consideration when going through the process. People who have experienced abuse, emotionally or physically, seem to have a pattern of initial denial. They project a positive image of the abusive person, sometimes to the point of idealizing him or her. I have heard this from many of my clients. I counseled an educated middle-aged man, who cried non-stop during a session discussing how his dad used to put him down, hit him, belittle him, and abuse his mom. My client, in a state of helplessness, would hide from this in a shadow of illusion that he believed would protect him. In this deceptive place, he felt safe, because the reality was so painful. Now, this gentleman was a normal functioning and intelligent human being professionally, but emotionally he had been blocked by his suppressed memories. But he was aware and wanted to help himself get out of that stage.

The problem with denial, if continued for too long, is that it will become a person's reality to a degree that he will become completely unaware of it.

Psychologists explain the grieving process as having a number of stages, ranging from shock, denial, anger, depression, and to acceptance. These stages are like grades in school. We cannot get to the next stage until we finish the prior one successfully. When there is a sense of loss, there is a feeling of grieving.

In an abusive situation, the abused person's sense of grief is due to the loss of love and affection that she is supposed to get from the abusive person; the person who is supposed to love her and nurture her. What follows is a sense of betrayal, whether it is by a parent or an intimate partner.

Bereavement means to be deprived by loss. After we lose something that is of value to us, we go through a process of grief. Numbness resulting from denial, anger, and sadness can be part of that process. Bereavement can also cause physical reactions, including sleeplessness, loss of energy, and loss of appetite.

Grieving is a normal process of life. We should embrace it rather than deny it, and accept the stages as they throw themselves at us. Being aware of them is the best cure of all. If we do not grieve a sense of loss, it will end up bottled inside us, causing blockages to self-growth. These bottled-up feelings may cause emotional or physical problems later in life. Processing and working through grief is a painful process, but it is essential to ensure future emotional and physical well-being. We should remember that there is no single way to grieve.

> For example, Marry said, in my situation I know that the process of grieving is a very personal process, and has been reflective of my identity, character, and level of maturity at the time of the loss. This is also true for my experiences with helping others grieve. The way we respond to grief may change over time, as we change. There is no set timetable for these stages, but there has to be a balance between them and the intensity of the loss.

Generally, it is not healthy to remain at one stage of the grieving process for too long. Feeling emotionally numb is often the first reaction to a loss, and may last for a few hours, days, or longer. This numbness can help us get through the realistic preparations for a life without the object of our loss. The next stage can be a combination of emotions, anger toward self and others, guilty feelings of "what if I'd done this," and blaming self or others for all problems. At this stage, one might need to withdraw from family and friends and have sudden outbursts of tears set off by good or bad memories. But, over time, if we acknowledge these feelings and this process, the pain and sadness will start to lessen. We will begin to see our life in a more positive light, still acknowledging that the feelings of loss may return. At the end, we learn to welcome our feelings as they come because they have a message for us that we need to listen to. We don't categorize feelings as bad or good, we categorize them as messengers.

Related to the emotional abuse, as mentioned before, these patterns of abuse are not limited to one culture, but are studied, prevented, and acknowledged more in Western society than in third-world countries. I had a Middle-Eastern client who was in the early stages of abuse, both emotionally and physically. She projected a positive image of her husband to herself and others, and believed that this image of him was true.

As her therapist, I could see that it was not real, but she was not ready to give up the imaginary figure that she had made up. She, like many others who go through abuse, was in a deep stage of denial and did not feel comfortable challenging herself by confirming her experience of abuse, and acknowledging what it was doing to her sense of self. She was not aware that the more she adapted to this state, the harder it would become to salvage her true unique self. She offered various explanations for her husband's negative behaviors.

At this stage, an abused will believe that controlling behaviors are caring behaviors, obsessions will be seen as love, and abuse will be seen as something that the abused deserves. Affairs will be seen as demonstrations of the sexual strength of the man who cheated, or the woman may think the infidelity was her fault because she did not pay enough attention to her husband. These illusions require much time to repair, to get the woman to a stage where she is ready to admit that there is a problem. Unfortunately, many don't take that route, believing that life "outside" of the marriage will be more difficult, and that the truth will condemn or ostracize them, instead of setting them free. In such a relationship, since the abuser is usually not confronted and is not ready to admit that a change is needed, the couple might stay the way they are and get used to their dysfunctional relationship without any attempt to find a solution.

Religion and Identity

Do I need to be religious? If so, why do I see so many people who call themselves religious but seem so disturbing in thought and life style? Why not just deny any form of religion and live free of it? Is spirituality different from being religious?

To be clearer about the concept of religion, we will start with Marry's character. Marry considers herself spiritual, not religious, in today's perspective but, unlike many, she seemed to be familiar with her religion's history and concepts. She did not deny it or it was not an unknown concept of her identity. She was familiar with its history and its origin from reliable sources not just by hearing it from others.

> Marry said, as a part of my identity search, I owed it to myself to learn what it means to be born a Muslim and into the religion of Islam, because this was another aspect of my being. It seems that since the tragedy of 9/11, racist views toward Islam have increased. Some associate terrorism with Islam, because the people who claimed responsibility for that attack identified themselves as Muslims.
>
> My understanding of Islam that it is a religion of the teachings of Mohammad, a seventh century Arab religious and political figure. There are reportedly about 1.4 billion Muslims today. The word Islam means submission, which is meant to

be submission to God. In Islam, Muhammad is not considered to be the founder of a new religion, but the accumulator of the fundamental faiths of Adam, Abraham, and other prophets whose messages had been misapprehend or dishonored over time. Islam, Judaism, and Christianity are all considered to be Abrahamic religions by Muslims.

The Middle East, South and Central Asia, and North Africa are among many parts of the world that practice Islam. Islam is also reported to be the second largest religion in many European countries, like France and United Kingdom. So, for a non-Muslim who may have racist views against this religion, it is well worth spending time to learn about it.

Once I started investigating the different religions of the world, I couldn't help but notice that they all seemed to be reflections of one another. This reflection manifested itself, on the surface, differently, depending on the time and place the religious laws were revealed, but the fundamental parts of all of them were the same. It's mortifying to realize that the reasons religious laws were introduced to people, which include teaching and helping them to be able to live with harmony and improve their lives, have now been devalued, allowing religion to be used by fanatics as a tool for damaging these processes of harmonization and improvement. These fanatics use religion to gain power or other personal gratification. They persuade their followers to believe that their way is the only right way, so that the followers, who are mostly vulnerable individuals, feel protected by thinking that they belong to a special group that will lead them somewhere extraordinary.

One's surroundings, senses, and perceptions are tools, which from the beginning of a person's life mold her existence as she goes forward. These form a person's experiences, which will accompany her throughout her life. Early experiences and learning play a crucial role in the person's later pattern of thinking, perception, and understanding. We should also consider the importance of genetic inheritance in one's interpretation and understanding of events. The role of heredity and genetics, and how they can predispose one to what steps she will take during her lifetime, cannot be underestimated.

We usually don't think of religion as something that is innate, but in reality it is. Religious traditions and customs form subconscious foundations for our thoughts and actions. Religious ceremonies become a part of our habits and behavior, and may often be seen as duties. We will act in accordance with our culture's traditions, and these contribute to the psychological elements that form our personality.

For a person who wants to be free in her choices, she must first learn to let go of these traditional ways of thinking, and free herself from them. To do that, she must learn to free her personality and character from addiction and entrapment in religious ceremonies and traditions. This process requires the person to go back to her unconscious memories, concealed within her mind, to learning created during her childhood, or even before her birth. Out of a successful untangling process comes a person who is a free human being, free from limitations and restrictions. It is, however, important to note that this type of freedom does not mean being thoughtless or inconsiderate, this type of freedom comes only after gathering knowledge and learning how to become self disciplined. It is only after achieving this true freedom that one can then begin to create a new groundwork for a reality that she can properly refer to as her own religious personality. (4) A life full of core values that truly works for her not out of imitation but out of application, learning and knowledge.

A thirteen century Sufi named Sheikh Najmeddin Kubra said about worship, "Worship is the abandonment of custom and habit." He further explained that religious duties are "striving toward knowledge without being imprisoned by duty, obligation, and limitation."(4)

It is not until you are truly free that you know what your obligations and duties are. You are not truly free until you learn who you are and what freedom means to you.

> Marry said, I was raised as a Muslim, and with traditions. I learned to free myself from them, and then learned to distinguish what was useful for me as a true method of self-discipline and growth, and what was simply replication of old traditions that were not useful to my mental and spiritual growth. I still find

myself being haunted by some of these old traditions, but at least now I am more aware of them and can catch myself. This process took me about two years to understand. It was one of the hardest steps I, personally, had to take in order to let go of the patterns of thinking that blocked me from growing. I had to walk away from the comfort zone that had turned into a stumbling block for my being.

In the Arabic language, God is named Allah, which is viewed as the same essence as that believed by Christians and Jews. The fundamental belief in Islam is that there is only one God (Towhid); one that is absolute, not relative. There are no visual metaphors or interpretation of God, because such visualization comes out of artistic personal minds and may lead one to an illusive adoration. Muslims believe that the Qur'an (or Koran) came to people through Mohammad. There have been discussions about whether these messages that were exposed to Mohammad came through his own unconscious functioning, or from some form of a divine foundation. In general, historians refuse to discuss this subject. I, personally, think they are both the same. When one becomes purely connected to one's soul, to one's true side, then one is able to be connected to his or her divinity.

Modern Western academics have reported that the Qu'ran of this time is very similar to the words Muhammad declared were revealed to him.

Mohammad went into a state of isolation from the world for a period of time before he received his revelation. It is interesting because this pattern of isolation for a period of time, is seen in a almost all major prophets and highly spiritual beings. It could be that they used this time to quiet their mind from all the thinking and just listen to the quietness inside. Mohammad was identified as "Mohammad Amin," which meant one who is honest. Muslim scholars diverge in opinion about Mohammad's character, and whether he made mistakes or committed sins during his life. The majority opinion is that Mohammad, and prophets in general, did not commit major sins, or what we call mistakes in today's world. The reason for it may be that they thought about a decision in great detail before acting on it and that they did not have as much irrational thought and emotional imbalance as an average person might have. They were functioning from their core self, or adult self, or a more mature form of a self.

The one thing that is noticeable to an informed mind is our inability to make a judgment and come up with a conclusion about what was considered to be moral hundreds of years ago, within the context of the intent of a prophet in the place and environment in which he lived.

Morality refers to the concepts of right vs. wrong, which is used in three frameworks:

1. An individual conscience, which is very personal, depending on the person's intentions. For example, a surgeon may use a knife to cut a patient's body to do surgery for cure, but a robber may use a knife to rob another person. They are both using knives and both are expressing the same behavior which is going through the slashing process, but one's intention is to save life and the other's is to destroy. The problem is that too many people make judgments based only on behaviors and not intentions. Most of us simply lack the ability to look deeper than the surface and see the real truth. That is why so much manipulation is happening in this word. Sometimes it seems like one has to learn how to say certain things and behave certain ways and get what one wants despite one's intentions.
2. The next one is the set of principles and judgments one holds, some of which are shared within the community.
3. The third one concerns the code of behavior (ethics) of the time and place in which the person lives.

In exploring Mohammad's life and his behavior, there was one thing that seemed clear to me, and that was that Muhammad had the distinctiveness of what psychologists call a self-actualized person. And that, by itself, is a process that seems to be a wonder, considering the time and place in which Muhammad lived. All the prophets, including Mohammad, had this characteristic in common. They manifested it differently, depending on the demands and maturity of their time and nation. They all followed their true self, which is a self that is the true reflection of creation, without attachments, unbalanced feelings, or irrational thinking; a self who knows and loves him and self and others, and is whole-heartedly walking through life to accomplish his or her mission. It seemed like they all functioned from their higher self, were in complete control of their behaviors, emotions, and thoughts. And their entire mission included guiding humanity not because they wanted attention, power, money, security or some other form of personal gain but because they believed that was what they were born to do. Nowadays, we see a large number of people who call themselves spiritual guidance, but if we gain the ability to look behind their surface, it becomes obvious that they are anything but. That is not to say there are none; there are certain people who gain the ability to become pure guidance. But it is our responsibility to learn from true sources.

When digging into the misunderstanding that exists in Islam, many misunderstandings between the followers of Islam have, I believe, originated from the important concept of Hadith. Hadiths are collections of Muhammad's sayings, by his followers. Hadiths are what seems to have caused so much diversity in today's Muslims' ways of thinking and living. The collecting of Hadiths did not begin until several generations following Muhammad's death. At the beginning of the first Islamic civil war (seventh century), people started to question the sources of Hadiths. For example, there were many "sequences of broadcast" in which X told Y who told Z. This process may have resulted in favoritism and predisposition in the original sayings. Many Muslims scholars became concerned about the validity of Hadiths and the possibility of their fabrication. These scholars developed a series of criticisms in an attempt to distinguish between an authentic saying and the fraudulent ones.

I have read and studied the Hadiths. At this point of my life, I feel somewhat confident to discern which ones make sense and which ones may have been fabricated, as I apply them to my personal life and decision-making processes.

The major part of Islam that I try to know about and learn about, in order to learn about my beliefs and its roots, are the five pillars. I consider Prophet Mohammad as a self actualized human who had transformed himself and had discovered these pillars to be useful tools. These are the core of Islam's regulations and commandments—the essence of Islam. These pillars caused a revolution in the Muslim world during the time of Prophet Mohammad. Some of the rest seem to me to be more personal views that have shaped the regulations.

These five pillars, along with Qur'an, personal knowledge, and self-discipline have been effective tools for me through this process of self-discovery. One of the most important tools has been my ability to learn new and diverse subjects. Becoming familiar with science from physic to astrology, biology, psychology, history etc has showed me how creation's laws and design works and how magnificent it really is.

I think we all need a set of core beliefs to focus on. Otherwise, we will get confused in this unlimited world. Once we find our true self, which is a self that is untouched, pure, and uncorrupted by childhood wounds and the implementation of groundless patterns of thinking, a self without the dust of deficiencies and environmental damages, a self that is honest to herself and knows its place in the world, a self that functions from its higher being and is more in control and aware of its different levels and its core, only then we can use these regulations to our benefit to get where we need to go, fulfilling our true self's needs, not our dusty self's desires. To use an example of how learning about my religion helped me, I investigated these five pillars of Islam, and this is what I learned, not based on imitation from others, but based on what made sense to me. These five pillars are:

1. Shahadat: Meaning that there is only one God and that Mohammad is a messenger. Everything is God. All the opposites that may seem to us as good or bad are of God, and within

him. God, to a true Muslim, is what nature is to a scientist, while in reality all are a part of this same Being called God. There is nothing that is considered to be outside this entity. The law of opposites that was described in the previous chapters is also a law that is within this entity. This reminds me of an astronaut who reported that once, moving away from earth, he was pointing to his city, then country, then continent, then earth, and then it just did not matter anymore.

2. Salat, or Communion: This is a form of meditation, relaxation, prayer, and showing gratitude for nature and its creator, the supreme. This is also giving some time off from daily life to reflect upon ourselves to see what progress we have made in life, both from a physical perspective and emotional/mental ones. In addition, this is a way for people who believe in this practice to get away from everyday life and focus on the absolute picture of life, putting their minds away from the anger and hatred, and any other negative feelings, toward another and shaping their minds into a more reasonable device which functions in balance between reason and feeling. Salat, done in its pure and appropriate form, is a complete form of meditation in which one uses a combination of verbal, physical, and mental forms of connecting with the whole Being. Salat is helpful for people to see themselves as a part of a greater picture in connection with others. Salat is a personal matter, depending on the level of one's maturity and ability to concentrate and understand the process. Many practicing Muslims have not been able to perform this act according to its true core. Some do it out of fear of afterlife punishment; some do it to ask for more and more personal gains; others do it out of imitation, or as a routine part of life, more like an addiction. True practitioners of this type of prayer are small in number. It seems like, in many ways, Salat has become more of a routine behavior with no positive outcome, rather than a way of connection to the world, purification of mind, and concentration.
3. Zakat, or Giving: This is helping the needy, helping them in any reasonable way one can, whether it is through wealth or other ways. According to Zakat, it is every human's responsibility to

help with the economic hardships of the society he or she lives in to reduce unfair inequality. It is also every human's duty to learn, increase knowledge, and share it with others. Prophet Muhammad always encouraged Muslims to educate themselves and increase their knowledge and understanding "from birth to death." That, he said, is the true freedom of self and connection to the ultimate. He also stated that the highest act of giving is educating others of the knowledge we've gained of the facts of life.

4. Sawn, or Fasting: Fasting is a way for Muslims to advance in disciplining themselves. It is a positive mental trainer to work on any addictive behaviors, including addiction to certain foods, as well as learning organizational skills. It is also a useful way to get on a diet and take control of eating patterns. During this month, Muslims are supposed to come together in harmony to celebrate and respect their bodies, minds, and beings, and to truly pay attention to and take care of themselves mentally and physically.
5. Hajj, or Pilgrimage to Mecca: This is a way for Muslims, at least once in their lifetime, to get together in harmony and peace, to feel a sense of belonging to a bigger group, and experience the sense of connectedness that it is supposed to bring about to people. However, it is unfortunate that many travelers report that they were not able to sense that feeling, due to witnessing incidents that opposed the intended message. For example, many report that pilgrims were pushing and shoving each other to get ahead of others, behavior which was contrary to the purpose of the trip—to worship in a spirit of connection and harmony.

Unfortunately, when it comes to using religion as a means for self-development, people often become religious for mistaken reasons, losing its principles altogether. These people practice, sometimes addictively, without benefiting from it in any way, certain religious rituals out of imitation of another person, without knowledge of why they are doing it.

A weak mind can easily be manipulated, using anything as the manipulation tool, whether religion or something else.

However, religion usually has the most power because it deals with the deepest aspects of being a human. Some people practice religious acts with the intent of gaining something during or after life. It's like being in a trading mechanism with this Being, which they have no knowledge of. Yet again, some practice religion to escape, most of the time temporarily, from a pain they are experiencing physically or emotionally, rather than finding the root of the problem for a true cure.

Rarely do you see a person who uses religion because of the love she feels toward her being and the superior creation, or as a tool to free herself from attachments, desires, and mental blockages. Rarely do you see religion as being used to liberate oneself.

Religion is, most importantly, supposed to be a tool to learn about self. True religious beliefs and practices can only be appreciated and taught by a person who is self-actualized, or by a seeker who is at a level of maturity where she can evaluate these beliefs accordingly, to get to her inner potential. Religious rules and laws cannot be interpreted by ordinary human beings who call themselves religious leaders. Most these people are functioning from a less mature form of their self; their need, need of money, power, attention, or other personal gains. As said, religion in its deepest and truest form is nothing more than a tool for an individual to become knowledgeable of him- or herself, and to become liberated.

I discussed self-liberation in both my previous books, ***Rumi & Self Psychology (Psychology of Tranquility)***, and ***Sara's Therapy: The way to Purity.*** To repeat some of that, in order to be a truly free person, we have to start with boundary and control; it can't be the other way around. In order to be able to do that, we may need some form of an authority to give us guidance and hope.

Take for example, the case of a small child. It's always discussed by psychologists how important it is for a child to have an environment in which there are both affection and discipline, in a balanced manner. Giving one without the other creates an emotionally and spiritually deficient human. The more discipline and self-control children are exposed to during their childhood, from authorities in their life who themselves are well balanced, the more those children are able to find a balance in future life as adults, and to be in control. The more affection children experience from their caregiver(s), the more they are able to express and experience themselves, their emotions, and their surroundings. The problem with today's world is that many individuals lack an environment in which both affection and discipline were provided, and becoming aware of this issue is an important first step in self-discovery.

Research shows that children who are from an environment that is either too restrictive or too relaxed are most likely to suffer from mental health issues, while children from a well-balanced, structured environment are less likely to suffer from these issues.

This is, in a way, true for us as adults too. We need to have some form of guidance to go by. Religion, in its pure, untouched form, can be a useful tool of guidance for an individual who wants to find her true self and her role in creation. But if it is not used properly and with full knowledge, it would be nothing but damaging. Maybe that's why we see so many misguided people who have become even more closed-minded because of following certain religious concepts. It is not the religion. It is the lack of knowledge about it that causes ignorance and being taken advantage of.

Many times we see people using religion as an excuse for prejudiced ways of thinking, and as a destructive force, due to the lack of knowledge they have about their own beliefs. We see many who kill others in the name of religion, who judge others, and don't seem to be able to be able to live with respect for and in harmony with others who have different views from them. We see too many miscategorizations, too many labels, too much violence, destruction, and ugliness using this concept. We get to a point where even the ones who were interested in learning about their religion and that of others, start having mixed feeling about this. I have heard it from too many people who were born Muslim, Jew, Christian, etc., "If those people are religious, then I want to stay away from it altogether."

They go and create new religious concepts to follow, and new and unknown groups are born, with their own new concepts of superiority, only way to heaven, etc. The cycle repeats itself, only in another form.

To use an example, Marry was asked about her feelings toward being a Muslim. She said that even though she is highly spiritual, she does not often tell people that she is religious because her way of being religious is different from what others think of being one today. She reported that she is more like a Sufi believer at this point.

> Marry used many examples, one of which was the term Jihad in Islam. Marry said that Jihad, in Islamic terms, means a struggle in the way of God, and is also sometimes used as a way to defend Islam and spread its words. Jihad's intent is not to convert non-Muslims to Islam, since Islam encourages that people should be free in what they choose. Rather, it is a tool to be used to expand and defend Islam. Notice the word defend is used, not attack. Defend is the process of planning to stop the enemy, while attack is a process of attempting to actively assault the enemy.
>
> Defending, in psychology, is equivalent to assertiveness, while attacking is equivalent to aggressiveness. Since all religions' intent is to bring harmony and peace on earth, they, in their true form, not what people are presenting, all forbid attacking, but encourage defending. The same concept is true in psychology for individuals. A person with a healthy sense of self should learn to be assertive, but not passive or aggressive. People should know their rights and be able to stand up and respect themselves. Therefore, killing innocent people is not Jihad; it is simply acting out of rage, anger, and violence all of which are forbidden in a true religious concept.

Conclusion

Many times during my seminars, people ask me about the one "solution."

My response is there are many solutions, depending on who you are.

First, find yourself, and then you will able to identify a solution that works for your problem. Anything you do before this stage of self-knowledge is a temporary pain reliever, like an analgesic medicine rather than a true and long-lasting cure. Analgesic medicine does not cure the disease, but makes the pain go away for a short time but it has side effects and the pain may resurface itself in another format. If one truly wants to restore oneself to health, one has to dig in, find the source of the problem, and be patient in the process of healing, which takes time. Many examples of mental and spiritual analgesics are seen every day—like people walking out of a group gathering saying that they have completely changed, only to go back to the same pattern of thinking and behaving.

The process of self-awareness is a life-long journey that takes time, energy, and focus.

During the process of self-discovery, one has to piece together different parts of his or her identity. Identity is like a puzzle. We have to find each piece, learn it, and put it where it belongs. That is the beginning of awareness; the rest of what we do before this stage is mostly a dream rather than an awakening.

Self-awareness is the understanding that one exists as an individual who is unique, and has valid personal thoughts and ideas. Self-awareness has always been a mystery in philosophical and scientific terms. In order to become a conscious being, one has to understand the foundation of his or her identity. This process helps a person know herself or himself objectively rather than subjectively.

Self-awareness is a contributing factor to the way people monitor their behavior and its effect on society and others. True cultural background is also an influential factor in the process of self-awareness, depending on what is valued the most, and which behaviors are considered by the culture to be viewed in a negative light.

Our minds have no boundaries or limits. With our minds, we can go anywhere in the universe. We can use them to destroy or to build. We can discover every piece of nature and how it functions, and we call it science. We can make all sorts of images and creations in our minds; we have the ability to travel through time using our thoughts. Physically, however, we are limited to space and time and certain conditions to be able to survive. So, what tools and methods do we need to have to be able to control and use this limitless mind in positive ways, rather than allowing it to be like a child running around with no purpose and motivation? How can we use this amazingly beautiful and powerful mind to create rather than to destroy?

The human state of mind (the spirit) can create the most sacred thoughts and actions, which are beneficial to everything. On the other hand, it can fabricate the most awful violence against people while labeling it as positive to reduce the feelings of guilt or shame, and to impose an deceptive form of pride or superiority. We see leaders guiding whole populations to do things that they would never do individually. These patterns of extreme coexistence of opposite parts of personality are seen only in humans. This could be because our actions are motivated by hope. At every stage of life, we have to have hope, to be able to move forward with determination. How we want to shape our minds and lead the thoughts produced by it and how we want to determine our hope is up to us. We are the creators of our own life and we are affecting life and being affected by it every second. It is time to be aware.

When it comes to ordinary questions of life, we have to consider that there is this central part, focal point, essence, spirit, soul, center, heat, nucleus, fountain, whatever one chooses to call it, within all of us that we have to focus on. If we keep ignoring it, we won't be able to get in tune with it. We have to work our way from inside out, not the other way around. We can't look around the world for things, people, places, etc. to make us happy. We have to find our core being, learn to love it, learn to know it, and only then we can know what will give us a sense of balance in life.

To have balance, one has to have a central point. We usually underestimate ourselves. We become slaves to our impulses and other people's not so pure intentions. We become weak minds who are easily manipulated by outsiders, whether it's someone who wants to sell to us something we don't need, someone who wants to make us believe s/he has something to offer that will make us happy, or others who think they can make better decisions for our life, not because they really want to help us, but because they have some sort of personal benefits in mind.

Too many times, we give in to our lower side. Too many times we get fooled by our ego or our sense of self, according to what we are trying to portray to the world. Too many times, we get manipulated because we lack knowledge. Too many times, our defenses blind us to the truth. Too many times, we take the phony as real. It seems like others pick for us what type of clothes we want to wear, what type of food we want to eat, and what type of car we want to drive. We make decisions based on imitation.

Isn't that what monkeys do? Aren't we above that? Aren't we humans with unlimited power? Aren't we the most evolved form of animals? So, why are we, sometimes, acting in ways that represent our lower, less evolved sides?

The more we learn, and apply what we learn, the more we are able to expand our minds. An expanded mind has less prejudiced views, more understanding, more reasonable views of the world, more tolerance of differences, is more assertive, and has more abilities to deal with the negatives or obstacles of life.

When we let ourselves live in a limited world in a soul that has been restricted and a slave to others, its surrounding, and its body, we stop our minds from learning new things. When we block ourselves from moving forward and settle for our lesser potential, we lose something, and that is the joy of growing and flowing to the fullest.

Sometimes, we just give up. We get engulfed in our negative memories, behaviors, and thoughts, and believe we are not worthy or capable of going any further. We focus on everyone around us except us. We may get addicted to something, whether positive or negative, just to escape this feeling of "there is a me that needs attention." It seems like there is an unspoken pain that we want to run away from. We step into this denial zone, and it may become our comfort zone. We are not willing to step out of it, anymore. We spend a lifetime in this zone, without ever questioning what was out there.

In the meantime, while we're being blocked, it seems like our core and soul can sense a chain that is keeping it from cultivating, maturing, and developing. It wants to remove the chain, but it's us that's not letting go. The chain can be anything from harmful behaviors to harmful thoughts and feelings which are rooted in the inability to step out of ignorance, the inability to acknowledge and process suppressed memories, and the inability to change. We start to feel emptier inside, while we may manage to find some kind of success outside and put all our focus and attention on it, not knowing that life is much more than that one aspect, and there is so much more to learn and experience. We may become a successful surgeon who is intellectually competent in his or her profession, but emotionally, spiritually, mentally he or she is as immature as a five-year-old. He or she simply stopped growing in all those other areas, and forgot that they ever existed.

That's why sometimes the same tools that can be used for us to grow from our core can become tools of obstruction. For example, our education, money, or career may feed our lower self and get us engulfed in a sense of superiority which will keep us in our comfort zone. If I'm superior, why would I want to move up?

We live in a world that easily attracts our senses to itself, if we live from impulses. When we live through our lower self, we are easily distracted and manipulated, and others decide for us what we need to live our lives, what to buy, how to dress, etc. We constantly find ourselves being drawn into new things that we're trained to think we "need" and can't live without. Our definition of change is not "moving upward," but "moving in a circle," only to go back to where we started.

For example, we keep on changing relationships, not to truly find a more fulfilling and satisfying one that helps us grow emotionally and spiritually, but to find one that gives only temporary satisfaction, which ends in a short run, and we find ourselves in the same dynamic as we were before. Another example would be that we keep changing jobs, only to find ourselves dissatisfied with each of them. We let others define for us what happiness is, without even knowing what it means for us to be happy.

It seems like we live in a world where we function and pay attention to the shallow much more than deep. Instead of working our way from core to surface, we work through the surface and forget about the core. That may be the root reason for so much stress, anxiety, depression, family problems, and an overall sense of inner dissatisfaction. It seems like we live in a world where so many people are just pretending, and functioning as if they are their persona or their masked self. To refer back to Marry and her experiences:

> Marry said, "I try very hard to belong to a group for socializing and sharing ideas. It seems harder and harder for me to find a group who can share my values."

Don't be afraid to go deeper. It's easy to allow superficialities such as race, religion, and politics to turn you off. Look beyond the obvious difference and seek greater truths. Remember, valuable things in life do not come easy. If we need to learn the truth, we have to put time and effort to explore. We need to walk throughout life learning and finding joy, since learning about the truth helps us find more joy and finding more joy increases our learning ability. So, they go hand in hand.

We need to learn to move beyond our conditioning and not be slaves of the outside world but a follower of our own inner guide. But first we have to access this inner guide by learning how to let go of the negative load we have been carrying. This negative load blocks our vision to the truth and makes our walk hard. This includes irrational thinking, unreasonable and immature emotions, and impulsive behaviors. When we let go of the unnecessary, we feel light, liberated and then we can see the truth and walk the walk.

Reference

1. Erickson, E., H. (1959). Identity and the Life Cycle. New York: International Universities Press.
2. Online Dictionary Source. Retrieved Jan14, 2007. http://dictionary.com
3. Maslow, A., H. (1998). Toward a Psychology of Being. Third Ed. New York: Wiley.
4. Economy Professor. Karl Marx. Retrieved July 12,2006. www.economyprofessor.com/theorists/karlmarx.
5. Sufism Journal. International Association of Sufism Publications. Vol.III, No.3.
6. Sebba, L., (1996). Third Parties, Victims and the Criminal Justice System. Ohio State University Press, Columbus.
7. Jahanian D. Iranian Women in the Avestan Period. Retrieved Jan 16, 2007. http://cais-soas/CAIS
8. Barirov, O., *The Origin of the Pre-Imperial Iranian Peoples*, accessed Jan 19, 2007.
9. Thomas, K., W., & Velthouse, B., A. (1990). Cognitive Elements of Empowerment: An 'Interpretive' Model of Intrinsic Task Motivation. Academy of Management Review, Vol 15, No. 4, 666-681
10. American Psychological Association Public Interest Directorate. Retrieved Sep/12/2006.

11. Dandamayev M. A., *Cyrus the Great*, from online source. http://www.cais/history
12. http://www.religioustolerance.org/isl_numb.htm retrieved Sep/12/06
13. http://www.firstchoicebooks.ca/pricing_main.htm
14. http://www.firstimpressionswriting.com/services.htm
15. http://heartsongbooks.com/tips2.html
16. http://www.childdevelopmentinfo.com/development/erickson.shtml
17. http://www.apa.org/pi/oema/racism/q03.html
18. A History of Iran: Empire of the Mind by Michael Axworthy

Other books by this author

<u>Book 1:</u>
Rumi & Self Psychology.
(Psychology of Tranquility)

Two astonishing perspectives for the discipline and science of self-transformation: Rumi's Poetic language vs. Carl Jung's psychological Language.

This book describes concepts like self respect, self liberation, self discipline, self assertion etc in a poetic and psychological language.

Book 2:
A Therapy Dialogue

A session-by-session therapy dialogue with an educated client who went through the self-actualization and self-growth processes. This book walks the reader through the process of therapy. In a step-by-step guide, it discusses what it means to live a life of "false self" and how to find a sense of "real self." It discusses a wide variety of issues like anxiety, family relationships, romantic relationships, negative behaviors and emotions and how to get rid of them, how to get to our full potential, what happiness really means, what is the difference between love and anxious attachment, what is assertiveness, how to process suppressed memories, and how to be able to see deeper into people's intentions, not just their behavior.

<u>Book 3:</u>

A concise comparison of theorists including Carl Jung and Abraham Maslow's concepts of the psyche and the self.

Finding a common ground between Carl Jung's general concepts of individuation, wholeness, spirituality and religion and those of Maslow's including his self Actualization and homeostasis concepts. (Out in 2010)

Book 4:
Where is my place in this world?

From egotistical to altruistic way of existence.

This book explains how to move above and beyond one's conditioning to get access to an unrepressed and infinite state of being where one can see that everything is inner connected and there is no separation. To get there one must increase her level of understanding and put her life to practice. The more one experiences life with awareness and knowledge, the closer she gets to her wholeness and that unlimited potential she beholds.

SKBF Publishing
Self Knowledge Base/Foundation Publishing

www.SKBFPublishing.com
Expanding your mind, widening your world, awakening your consciousness, and enhancing your life; one book at a time.

SKBF Publishing is a publishing company dedicated to providing educational information for enhancing lifestyles and helping to create a more productive world through more aware individuals. Our task is to help awareness overcome ignorance. Our publishing focus is on research-oriented and/or reliability contented books, including subjects related to education, parenting, self-improvement, psychology, spirituality, science, culture, finance, mental and physical health, and personal growth. We try to analyze each book carefully and to choose the books we feel have reliable and valid information based on available research or the credentials of the author. Our team of experts review every manuscript submitted to us for its practicality and content.

Our mission is to publish information that expands understanding and promotes learning, compassion, self-growth, and a healthy sense of self which leads to a healthier lifestyle. Our vision is to make a difference in people's lives by providing informative material that is reliable or research-oriented. SKBF Publishing is honored to have the helping hand of a number of scientist, educators, researchers, intellectuals, and scholars working together to review the books before approval for publishing with SKBF.

About the Author

Dr. Rohani Rad has a Doctorate in Clinical Psychology and a Masters e in Applied Psychology. She is a member of American Psychological Association (APA), Virginia Psychological Association, and Applied Psychological Association.

In addition, she is the founder of a not-for-profit foundation (www.SelfKnowledgeBase.com) with the sole task of bringing awareness to a wide variety of subjects ranging from root-oriented understanding of global peace to child abuse. This foundation aims to be a bridge of understanding between the East and the West by generating research-oriented material and awareness.

Dr. Rad is also a researcher, and is actively involved with a number of studies related to emotional wellbeing, children's mental health, and relationships, among others. These studies are performed in both the Eastern and the Western sides of the globe for a broader perspective of factual information.

Dr. Rad has written a number of recognized and up-to-the-point books about the subjects of self-discovery, self-growth, and self-awareness from a psychological perspective. You can find more information about the author and her books on her website at www.OnlineHealthClinic.com

My God

Don't limit my God
Don't give her a façade

My God is not a God of deprivation
He does not belong to one particular station

My God is a combination
There is no separation

My God is an unrestrained totality
Anything lesser is just my reality

My God gave me an active voice
My God granted me free choice

Poem by Roya R. Rad

Self Value

You turn into what you hear
So sort out what goes in your ear

You turn out to be what your eyes observe
So ensure what you see is what they deserve

You grow to be what you've believed
So make certain you are not being deceived

Your free choice can take you to infinity
Do you choose the edge or the divinity?

You become with whom you interact
So make sure you know whom to attract

When you get rid of useless distraction
You gain a sense of inner satisfaction

You appreciate what is vital
You let go of the shallow title

Poem by Roya R. Rad